June 1979

Congratulations, Stephen.
Continue your sustained effort next year.

Have a great summer!
Margaret McGrath
(Principal)

A Pictorial History of Radio in Canada

Sandy Stewart

Gage Publishing Limited
Toronto

TABLE OF CONTENTS

Introduction   v

IN THE BEGINNING WAS THE WORD   1

HOW GOD CREATED THE CBC
     (with a little help from his friends)   11

RADIO'S COPPER AGE   1906-1936
     Ah, ah, ah . . . Don't Touch that Dial   29
     And Now for a Word from   43
     The Next Sound You'll Hear   53

RADIO'S SILVER AGE   1936-1949
     Radio Rallies Round the Flag   67
     Radio and the Stars . . . Trade Secrets Revealed!   97

RADIO'S GOLDEN AGE   1944-1954
     Hello Out There in Radioland!   113
     Signing Off   147

BIBLIOGRAPHY   150

INDEX   152

To my wife Pat

Introduction

On December 12, 1901 radio made its official beginning in North America — and there were Canadians involved. They have remained involved ever since, broadcasting across greater distances than any other country in the world. Canadian radio also produces more programs, operates more networks and serves its listeners better than any other nation.

How did this proud history take place? In typical Canadian fashion, through the invention of an Italian, the use of British money and on Newfoundland real estate. Even more typically, the brilliant Canadian radio inventor, Reginald Fessenden, was effectively frozen out of his own country by Marconi and had to leave Canada to pursue his career in the United States. This was and has remained the pattern of Canadian radio ever since. The major books on Canadian broadcasting — *The Politics of Canadian Broadcasting* by Frank Peers and *The Struggle for National Broadcasting in Canada* by Austin Weir — deal thoroughly with nationalist frustrations in the world of Canadian radio. This pictorial history will therefore avoid dwelling on this part of our history and focus instead on Canadian achievements in radio. There are many.

As a broadcaster in both the private and public sector, I've enjoyed the challenge of studying our radio history but I have been blocked by two major obstacles. Most broadcasters are far too busy to worry about the past. They regularly throw out old scripts, photographs and program material as they relentlessly pursue their new ideas. The CBC has never established effective policies to ensure the preservation of its historical records, nor has the private radio sector. I hope that this book will stimulate interest in radio history. I intend to continue gathering material from any and all sources and I urge anyone with useful material to send it to me at the CBC, Box 500, Terminal A, Toronto, Ontario. After extracting information from such material I will forward it to the National Archives in Ottawa.

While the basic information in this book is from weekly publications, the details — the humor, the romance — come from the people who were involved in the programs. I was overwhelmed by their co-operation, generosity and hospitality. If there are omissions in this book it is because there are far more programs, anecdotes and personalities than can be contained in one book. It was a privilege to have been associated with these people during my radio career. I hope they enjoy this small history as much as I enjoyed writing it.

v

AN UNSUNG HERO   *Reginald Fessenden, the Canadian inventor of radio telephony.*

IN THE BEGINNING WAS THE WORD

I f Canadian radio archives do not contain as much material as they should, there is one historical event well documented — the achievement of Guglielmo Marconi, an Italian who made radio history by transmitting the letter "s" in Morse code from Poldhu, Cornwall, England to a receiving station on Signal Hill overlooking St. John's Harbour in Newfoundland on December 12, 1901.

But an equally historic event, the achievement of a brilliant Canadian inventor, Reginald Aubrey Fessenden, is generally ignored and largely unknown. On December 24, 1906, at 9 P.M. eastern standard time, Reginald Fessenden transmitted human voices from Brant Rock near Boston, Massachusetts to several ships at sea owned by the United Fruit Company.

The host of the broadcast was Fessenden. After giving a résumé of the program Fessenden played a recording of Handel's "Largo" on an Ediphone thus establishing two records — the *first* recording on the *first* broadcast. Fessenden then dazzled his listeners with his talent as a violinist playing appropriately for the Christmas season, "Oh Holy Night" and actually singing the last verse as he played. Mrs. Helen Fessenden and Fessenden's secretary Miss Bent, had promised to read seasonal passages from the Bible including, "Glory to God in the highest and on earth peace to men of good will," but when the time came to perform they stood speechless, paralyzed with mike fright. Fessenden took over for them and concluded the broadcast by extending Christmas greetings to his listeners as well as asking them to write and report to him on the broadcast wherever they were.

The mail response confirmed that Fessenden had successfully invented radio as we know it. Technically, he had invented radio telephony or what radio listeners would call "real" radio as opposed to Marconi's Morse code

1

Marconi

×

Hamper contains balloon

Marconi's team inside Cabot Tower, Signal Hill, St. John's, Newfoundland, where radio history was made.

broadcasting. Fessenden could truly lay claim to be the inventor of radio and he fully expected the world to beat a path to his door. Instead, he never received his due recognition, lost control of his patents and the ensuing revenue which made other inventors and companies immensely wealthy. Even today the *Encyclopedia Canadiana* does not give him a separate listing. Mention of him is only included under the listing for his mother Clementina who established Empire Day in Canada. Reginald is mentioned as one of her four sons, "inventor of the wireless telephone, the radio compass and the visible bullet for machine guns, he also invented the first television set in North America in 1919."

Unlike Marconi who received a grant from the Canadian government to continue his experiments in Cape Breton, Fessenden was neither a good businessman nor an accomplished promoter. Born in 1866 near Sherbrooke, Quebec, he received his education in Canada but left to work in the field of electricity in the United States. He became chief chemist for Thomas Alva Edison who was developing his power company at that time and later left to

Fessenden (seated) and staff at Brant Rock operations.

work for George Westinghouse. Westinghouse, impressed with Fessenden's brilliance, agreed to make instruments and machines for him when he left his employ to become head of the electrical engineering department of the University of Pennsylvania. Fessenden in turn was to remain available to Westinghouse for research. It was an excellent deal for both and gave Fessenden the chance to work on the theories of Henrich Hertz of Karlsruhe who had studied electromagnetic waves and discovered they could travel through walls. Many young inventors of the time were also frantically studying Hertz's theories in the hope of improving on the Morse Telegraph System by developing a wireless version. The race was on and Fessenden was in it.

But in 1896 Marconi's successful experiment on Salisbury Plains in the U.K. where he transmitted a radio signal netted the inventor £76,000 from the British government for the patent. Discouraged because Marconi seemed to be leading the race, Fessenden took off for a long holiday near Peterborough, Ontario. His radio ideas had dried up on him and he was thoroughly depressed. It was while he was daydreaming beside a lake during his holiday that the ripples on the lake spreading out from a stone he had dropped, gave him the idea he needed. What if sound waves travelling out from the centre were continuous like the ripples on the lake?

Fessenden was on the right track and nine years later he'd prove it. Rejected by McGill in favour of an American professor for the university's vacant electrical engineering chair he returned to his Pennsylvania job and worked furiously on his new theory. It was during this period that by accident his assistant, Mr. Kitner, jammed a Morse code key which howled over a receiver and was transmitted to Fessenden in another room. Fessenden concluded that if the howl could be carried voices could too, and he decided that what was needed were very fast controlled waves of high frequency which would carry sounds. Fessenden theorized that the fast frequency could be broadcast with program information, and a receiver could isolate the program information from the carrier and leave sound for his listeners. Fessenden knew that his previous experience in electrical engineering while working for Edison and Westinghouse would help him to design and build a high-speed generator or dynamo to carry his information. If he could get a steady enough set of radio waves he knew he could put voices or music "on the air". But he needed a lot of money to design and build his generator and most of all he would need time—he would have to leave his university work and concentrate on his inventions if he was to prove his theories.

In order to make some money, he demonstrated the telegraph equipment which he'd been developing at the University to the United States Weather Bureau and sold them on the use of radio (with future improvements), for weather forecasting. He figured he could develop transmitters and receivers for the u.s. Weather Bureau and at the same time develop his other theories while using their generators. His Morse system functioned on primitive slow speed generations but Fessenden had convinced his new employer that a faster and better generator would do a better job for Uncle Sam. Fessenden's deal included retaining the ownership to his design and inventions.

Fessenden's new lab was at Cobb Island in the Potomac River, where he was experimenting with a receiving station at Arlington Virginia, fifty miles away. He and his assistant Thiessen had perfected Morse transmissions using a new generator they had bought, and in October of his first year Fessenden experimentally hooked up a microphone to the improved system. On December 23, 1900 Fessenden said into his microphone, "One, two, three, four. Is it snowing where you are Mr. Thiessen? If so telegraph back and let me know."

Thiessen replied by telegraph in Morse code that it was indeed snowing. In great excitement Fessenden wrote at his desk, "This afternoon here at Cobb Island, intelligible speech by electromagnetic waves has for the first time in World's History been transmitted." This was almost a year before Marconi's transmission in Morse code from England to Signal Hill in Newfoundland, on December 12, 1901.

Fessenden's employers, the u.s. Weather Bureau, were pleased and Willis Moore, Fessenden's boss, suggested he move his experiments to North Caro-

Fessenden working with his Baretter invention. Note disciplined layout of equipment.

lina to experiment between Cape Hatteras, Roanoke and the mainland, a hundred-mile triangle. But things now began to go sour for Fessenden. On December 12, 1901 Marconi successfully transmitted across the Atlantic Ocean to St. John's, Newfoundland. Fessenden had wanted to beat Marconi and again he had failed. His employer, Willis Moore of the u.s. Weather Bureau was trying to shake down Fessenden for a share of his patents and this was causing strain as well. Fessenden complained to Theodore Roosevelt, without success, and in August, 1902 Fessenden left his job and went to Bermuda where his wife's family lived.

Fessenden was now forced to continue his search for financial backing for his experiments. He approached the Canadian Government which had already spent $80,000 supporting Marconi at Glace Bay, but was refused. So back to the u.s. he went where he teamed up in Pittsburg with two millionaires, Given and Walker, to form the National Electric Signalling Company, and built two wireless stations near New York City on each side of Chesapeake Bay, later adding three more at New York, Philadelphia and Washington.

Despite his setbacks Fessenden was making tremendous strides in Morse code transmission and the company now held an enormous number of American patents. He was also gaining a worldwide reputation as a scientist, but unlike Marconi he remained a lone-wolf experimenter. Even though Marconi's successful transmission across the Atlantic had resulted in both publicity and adulation for the Italian scientist, Fessenden was convinced that Marconi's "whiplash" method, an "on and off" type of transmission, did not work well enough. Most researchers were pursuing the "whiplash" idea because they could not accept the idea that electromagnetic continuous waves could be created, loaded with a program, transmitted and then eliminated leaving only the program for the listeners. Fessenden's mathematical background made this abstract idea easy for him to grasp. Other inventors who had not had his training were still fumbling along for solutions without any real knowledge of exactly where they were heading.

Meanwhile, the next major step for the National Electric Signalling Company was to build radio transmission towers at Brant Rock near Boston and in Scotland for trans-Atlantic experiments. Despite his disappointments in Canada Fessenden remained a true patriot and rather than transmitting from the u.s. he wanted to transmit between Canada and Europe. So on July 20, 1906, by an act of Parliament, Fessenden formed a Canadian company supported by Sir Robert Borden and other influential men, called the Fessenden Wireless Telegraph Company of Canada. Canada was now sewn up by Fessenden but there were other problems at the radio station at Machrihanish in Scotland. The technicians involved couldn't seem to get the hang of the equipment and the station could not receive even over short distances. Fessenden was furious. He was so confident that the fault was with the technicians and not with his plans that he sent Armour, his best engineer, to Scotland to take over while he continued his local experiments in the u.s. and did the paper work required to clean up his 300 patents.

At about this same time Fessenden was also learning a little about the effect of weather conditions on radio broadcasts. He'd been experimenting enough to know that cold weather and long nights were good times to transmit and that warm weather during daylight time was poor or impossible. On the night of January 3, 1906 the weather was ideal—cold and dark. Fessenden adjusted a gadget on his transmission tower which resembled an umbrella frame and started transmitting Morse code to Armour in Scotland. Later that night a cable arrived saying "We are getting you Brant Rock, loud and clear." It looked as if things were beginning to jell for Fessenden now—he had finally perfected an invention similar to Marconi's but more reliable and less slap-dash. It wasn't reliable enough, though, to work through the following spring, and there still remained problems to iron out.

When the cold and dark weather returned in the fall he resumed his Trans-

Early wireless telegraphy. Note wires strung everywhere compared to Fessenden's orderliness.

Atlantic Morse experiments and his local voice experiments, and in November he received a "personal" registered letter from his engineer, Armour, at Machrihanish which both delighted and shocked him. The letter said, "at about 4 o'clock in the morning I was listening in for telegraph signals from Brant Rock when to my astonishment I heard instead of dots and dashes, the voice of Mr. Stein telling the operators at Pymouth how to run the dynamo. At first I thought I must be losing my senses, but I'm sure it was Stein's voice for it came in as clearly as if he were in the next room."

Fessenden frantically checked the logs which recorded the various tests and satisfied himself that he'd actually invented equipment which could and did transmit voices across to Scotland. It had been a happy accident, but another accident now took place which stopped Fessenden cold. A storm wrecked his Scottish receiving tower on December 6, 1906.

Marconi (fig. to far left) raising his kite at Signal Hill, St. John's, Newfoundland where the first wireless transmission was received from across the Atlantic, December 12, 1901.

There was still another shock in store for Fessenden. He learned that Marconi had been given exclusive rights to build wireless stations in Canada. So much for Fessenden and his Canadian company. The idea that Marconi, an Italian received not only the approval but support of the Canadian government which Fessenden, a Canadian, had been denied, infuriated and frustrated the inventor. He *had* to prove his genius, prove to the world and Canada that he was the real inventor of radio.

He held a contract with the United Fruit Company which had installed wireless systems on the boats to control the harvesting and marketing of bananas in Puerto Rico, and Professor Fessenden decided to give a Christmas present to his customers on the dozen or so ships of the United Fruit Company at sea. He told the wireless operators to listen on Christmas Eve for "something different". At 9 o'clock the operators heard the familiar "C.Q." which means "listen all stations" from Brant Rock and then they heard Fessenden's voice speaking.

On that cold December night Fessenden knew he had given the world one of the greatest Christmas presents it would ever receive. Without wires across vast distances, he had transmitted human voices. The word was made known and Fessenden truly believed the world was now at his feet.

Instead, the rest of Fessenden's life was a constant struggle for recognition for his inventions and compensation from his rich partners who had sold his patents out from under him to large American companies. Fessenden returned to Canada from time to time but he never settled here again and died finally, relatively unknown, in Bermuda. American books that do condescend to recognize Fessenden's achievement describe him as the "American Marconi". Perhaps it is just as well he never had the chance to read that.

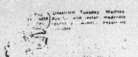

New York American

EDITION FOR   GREATER NEW YORK

TUESDAY, APRIL 16, 1912. 16 PAGES   PRICE ONE CENT In Greater New York: Elsewhere and Jersey City TWO CENTS

BUSINESS PROPERTY
TO LET. The best Variety in Every Section of the Advertised Every Day and Sunday in AMERICAN "WANT AD" PAGES

J. J. ASTOR LOST ON TITANIC
1,500 TO 1,800 DEAD

John Jacob Astor was among the passengers who went down with the ship, according to a wireless dispatch received by Bradstreets last night from the liner Olympic.   Mrs. Astor was saved and is being brought to shore by the Carpathia.

The Wireless Operator at Cape Race, Newfoundland, Flashes: "Eighteen Hundred Lives Have Been Lost in the Wreck of the Titanic."

The Titanic as she rammed the iceberg. Drawn from the wireless reports of the disaster.

Vice-President P. A. S. Franklin, of the White Star Line, said:

"We have heard the rumor from Halifax that the three steamers—the Virginian, Parisian and Carpahia—stood by the Titanic.

"We have received a wireless from Captain Haddock, of the Olympic, that the Titanic went down at 2.20 a. m.

"We have also heard indirectly that the Carpathia has 675 passengers aboard.

"The total passengers and crew on the Titanic numbered 2,000.

"It is very difficult to say whether the Virginian and the Parisian have any survivors aboard until we get a direct report. We have asked for that report from our Halifax agent and from others."

Carpathia Proceeding Directly to New York

The Carpathia is proceeding direct to New York. We very much fear there has been a serious loss of life. But it is impossible at this time to assure ourselves that the other steamers have or

Continued on Page 2.

More than 1,500 persons, passengers and crew, perished yesterday when the "unsinkable" Titanic, the $10,000,000 White Star liner, went to the bottom of the sea.

So report the steamers which, in answer to the Titanic's wireless shrieks for help, "Hurry! hurry!" rushed to her aid. There is little hope that the dread report is not true.

Of the 2,200 souls who were aboard the once mighty ship 675 were saved.

As The New York American told yesterday, the Titanic, the largest, most luxurious—vaunted as the safest—steamer that ever sailed the seas, collided with an iceberg at 10:45 P. M., Sunday, in about latitude 41.46 North and longitude 50.14 West.

That is, the ill-fated boat was about 1,200 miles east of Sandy Hook and about 900 miles southeast of Halifax, N. S.

Twentieth Century Triumph in Ship Building

The Titanic was the Twentieth Century triumph of shipbuilding. Yet

HOW GOD CREATED THE CBC
(with a little help
from his friends)

When the Titanic sank to her watery grave on the night of April 14, 1912 it marked the end of one era and the beginning of another, a time when radio would be recognized as a medium of communication of far-reaching importance. Before the Titanic disaster early radio had been considered only commercially useful and was used primarily for shipping. As radio waves travel more readily over open sea this had been a natural development, although there was the odd person thinking further ahead.

There is a report that at the end of 1906 when Fessenden made his Christmas broadcast he invited important witnesses to the broadcast including the editor of the *American Telephone Journal*. In the next edition of the *Journal* the editor wrote: "At sea the wireless telephone may be used as a safety device in foggy weather. On land, it is doubtful if it will ever supplant the local exchange with wires. It is admirably adapted to the transmitting of news, music etc. as owing to the fact that no wires are needed, simultaneous transmission to many subscribers can be affected as easily as to a few." This prophet was thinking in terms of wireless telephone while the rest of the world was either ignoring radio or adapting it to marine use.

Although Marconi's system had been used as early as 1899 to save a light ship off the English coast, the single event which brought radio emphatically to the forefront of public consciousness was the tragedy of the Titanic, thirteen years later. As befitted the most modern ship ever built, the Titanic had been equipped for her maiden voyage to North America with the best available equipment including a Marconi transmitter and Marconi telegrapher. When this modern ship struck an iceberg and it quickly became obvious that the "unsinkable" ship was indeed going to sink the telegrapher immediately sent out a distress message "COD, SOS from MGY" (call of the Titanic) "We've struck a berg. Sinking fast. Come to our assistance. Position, Latitude 41.46 north, longitude 50.14 west MGY". Several ships heard the signal and the Carpathia, 58 miles away, rushed to the scene only to find lifeboats and rafts where the

11

BETTMANN ARCHIVE

In a dramatic pen and ink drawing of the period (below) Titanic survivors thank their saviour Signor Marconi, inventor of the wireless telegraph.

A 1912 drawing of the Titanic striking the iceberg (above) illustrates how the underwater portion of the berg sliced the hull below the waterline in a 300 foot sweep rendering the watertight compartments useless. The icy Atlantic flowed down into those left.

BETTMANN ARCHIVE

ship had gone down at 2:20 A.M. ninety-five miles south of the Grand Banks of Newfoundland. When the ship sank 1,513 people died but 711 had been rescued because of the radio message sent by Jack Phillips, the Titanic's telegrapher.

On the rescue ship Carpathia the low-powered radio was again used to send the horrifying news of the disaster to the mainland. Other ships helped out but there was some real danger that the competition for information was confusing the airways. President Taft ordered all radio stations in the U.S. to go off the air so that the weak signals from sea could be more easily heard and reported. David Sarnoff, student and employee of Marconi's, had a radio set in Wannamaker's department store in New York, and for seventy-two hours he sat translating the names of the survivors from Morse code to English.

← antenna

receiver

morse code key

ck Argyle
adio
ngineer

J. O. Cann

XWA, the world's first scheduled radio station, is now CFCF, Montreal.

Along with Marconi, Sarnoff received great acclaim for his help, rapid promotion in the Marconi Company and became the head of the Radio Corporation of America when R.C.A. absorbed the American Marconi Company in 1919. Sarnoff deservedly got credit but he was not the only telegrapher involved in this monumental use of radio. Charles B. Ellsworth, a seventeen-year-old Marconi telegrapher was based at station MCE, Point Riche, Cape Race, Newfoundland, and he also translated the tragedy from the Titanic and relayed the messages to the mainland.

However, although the sinking of the Titanic proved the importance of radio to sea-going ships, control of the new medium still remained mainly in the hands of experimenters. But in 1917 when the U.S. got involved in the First World War the United States Government seized control of all the radio patents in the country for war purposes thus ending a commercial struggle which had been going on for some time among inventors. After the war the

13

Pittsburgh's KDKA (above) claimed to be North America's first radio station but XWA, Montreal, was actually the first.

Frank Mullen, first American newspaperman to double as a radio commentator, speaking into a tomato-can mike.

NOTE SOAR BOX
(a prophesy?)

A 1920 photo of KDKA's first radio transmitter.

opportunity then existed to consolidate radio under an amalgamation of most patent holders including Westinghouse, General Electric and the American Telegraph and Telephone Company. They formed the Radio Corporation of America which effectively controlled the manufacture of broadcast equipment for some time after that in the United States.

Meanwhile, in Canada, Marconi was competing for another radio "first". While the Americans claim that KDKA, Pittsburg was the first radio station in North America, a legitimate counterclaim can be made for Marconi's station XWA in Montreal. Both stations were experimenting with broadcasts to local "hams" in 1919. No record appears to have been kept as to the first time a transmission was received from either of these stations by an audience. Things didn't happen that way nor should they.

However, if a scheduled broadcast is accepted as a starting point, Canada's XWA beat out the American KDKA. The first scheduled broadcast in North America was a musical program relayed on May 20, 1920, from XWA in Montreal to a meeting of the Royal Society of Canada in Ottawa. The first scheduled broadcast on KDKA in Pittsburg, Pennsylvania, was a broadcast of the Harding-Cox presidential election returns on November 2, 1920. Meanwhile in other countries such as Holland and England similar broadcasting stations were also going on the air.

15

Alice Brady

4827-12

▲ *An artist performing in front of a "dishpan" mike in the early 1920s.*

◀ *In this 1925 radio photo, the mike is hidden in the standard lamp.*

17

The first broadcasts to lure Canadian listeners away from American programs were Foster Hewitt's Saturday night hockey broadcasts.

By the late 1920s radio had become a fact in the livingrooms of wealthy North Americans and most of them were listening to the big American stations. The Canadian stations operating at that time were not doing much business for two reasons: The Canadian Government's indifference towards financing radio broadcasting prohibited big Canadian stations and the Canadian radio programming was not significantly different from American programming which did it better.

Early radio sets were decorated like living rooms to make guests and performers feel at home.

It was hockey which first convinced Canadians to listen to their radio stations. In the u.s. "going to the movies" had become the Saturday night pastime, but in Canada there were not as many movie houses available to a widely scattered population and so Canadians stayed home to listen to the radio. Since almost everybody in the u.s. was at the movies on Saturday nights the American broadcasters often didn't bother to list the evening's programs, but in Canada General Motors sponsored the Saturday night hockey broadcasts. Canadians tuned in and hockey became as Canadian as maple syrup and still is. Foster Hewitt, only one of several young broadcasters who reported hockey games on radio also became as national an institution as the game itself because of his unique talent.

However, despite the success of the hockey games Canadians still continued to listen to American stations for all other programs. American shows

 Darby Coats (standing) teaches radio operators at the Marconi School in Montreal in 1919.

of the time with large Canadian audiences were General Motors, General Electric, R.C.A. Victor, Atwater Kent, The Camel Hour and Cities Service starring Jessica Dragonette. Then, on October 29th, 1929, the great stock market crash plunged North Americans into the Depression. The free entertainment on radio became even more attractive to Canadians forced to stay home because they were broke or jobless. But there was still no Canadian radio to speak of except for the Canadian National Railway network which did an excellent job but was on the air for only a few hours each week.

The reason there was so little Canadian programming was the continuing indifference of the Canadian government toward the new communication medium. Although the government collected license fees—$50 for commercial stations, $5 for amateurs and $1 for receivers—the revenue went into the

Churches quickly discovered radio was effective for preaching the gospel.

Federal pocket for other purposes than radio except in Manitoba where the province used part of the fees to support CKY and CKX. The Americans, on the other hand, had never bothered with radio license fees and had managed to develop excellent radio—radio that Canadians listened to.

By 1928 however, funding for Canadian radio began to come from an unexpected source, the churches. Radio had become an important element in religion. One private station in Montreal which had folded was revived by a group of ministers to preach the Gospel, and in Vancouver there were three religious stations; one of them owned by the National Bible Students Association of the Jehovah's Witnesses. The Witnesses also had stations in Edmonton, Saskatoon and a phantom station in Toronto, used extensively under the call letters CFCX. Two other religious stations in Toronto were CJBC for Jarvis

Street Baptist Church and another for the Roman Catholic St. Michael's Cathedral.

But in 1927 and early 1928 the Department of Marine began to receive a great number of complaints about the broadcasts by the Jehovah's Witnesses. An excerpt taken from one of the broadcasts indicates why:

"We know that all true followers of Christ Jesus are now united under the King, the Greater David, and that these are loudly proclaiming Jehovah, his King, and his Kingdom. Heretofore the Roman Catholic Hierarchy has had its own way. It has been a great test to the true followers of Christ Jesus. That wicked organization, acting under the pretext of being God's representatives on earth, has crushed every organization that has ever risen against it. Now, Christ is on his throne and God's time has come to put his kingdom completely in control under Christ, the Roman Catholic Hierarchy has begun and carries on its assaults against God's true people. In every country of earth the Hierarchy carries forward this wicked persecution . . ."

To complicate matters the Witnesses had lost control of one of their stations which had gone commercial and rented air time to the Ku Klux Klan in Saskatchewan. The Minister, the Honourable P. J. A. Cardin, decided to take action. He quietly switched frequencies across the country, forcing some stations off the air. Four of the stations were owned by the Witness Bible Students Association and they began to raise a terrestial hell that rocked the country. To add to their fury, one of the reallocated frequencies had gone to a distillery, Gooderham and Worts and they charged that as well as discriminating against them, the Liberal government preferred booze to the Bible. Five thousand watts of religious indignation now hit the air, Parliament and the press.

When the subject was debated in Parliament, the Conservatives made the most noise but the Labour member from Winnipeg North, J. S. Woodsworth, made the most sense. He wanted to know just when the minister, Mr. Cardin, had been appointed censor of religious opinion. Mr. Woodsworth suggested that perhaps the Orange lodges and the Catholic churches should be censored along with the Witnesses. The whole freedom of religion issue led into a discussion on how these problems were being dealt with in other countries, and how to give radio audiences the programs they wanted. With the pressures building up, Mr. Cardin did what Canadian politicians who make mistakes still do—he appointed a Royal Commission to look into broadcasting policies around the world and to recommend a system for Canada.

The Royal Commission chairman was Sir John Aird, president of the Canadian Bank of Commerce. The other commissioners were Charles Bowman, editor of the Ottawa Citizen, and Dr. August Frigon, a Montreal electrical engineer. They did a thorough study of the situation and reported back to Mr. Cardin September 11, 1929. The report was concise—only nine pages long.

Early sound lock studio door

NBC performers standing at decorated music mike in the 1920s while commentator sits at double announcer's mike.

It objected to the dominance of American radio stations across Canada and recommended a Public Service broadcast system either of groups of subsidized private-stations or of a national system financed federally or provincially. It was to be called the Canadian Radio Broadcasting Company. The Commission wanted seven high-powered radio stations across Canada, and recommended a $3 receiver license fee for listeners. It also recommended a $1,000,000 annual subsidy for the c.r.b.c. and advised that the new company not carry any advertising. If put into effect these policies would eliminate private broadcasting and also remove a large number of newspapers from broadcasting as well as a lot of sponsors from marketing through radio.

The first general reaction from the press in Canada was favourable and supported the Aird report and the Liberal government began to prepare the bill for the legislature. But during the delay before the bill came down the broadcasters and newspapers began to have second thoughts and Edward Beatty, president of the CPR decided private enterprise could do a better job

Thomas Maher

W. Arthur Steele

R.P. Landry (secretary) Hector Charlesworth

The Canadian Radio Broadcasting Commission (above) was formed in 1932 because of a freedom-of-religion issue.

than the national system recommended by Aird. Then in 1930 Mackenzie King informed his cabinet he was calling an election which stopped the act from getting into the house. In the election, broadcasting was not an issue but the Liberal party was defeated and Mr. Bennett and his Conservative colleagues formed the next government.

The Canadian Broadcasting Act of 1932 which was introduced by the Conservative Prime Minister R. B. Bennett was a remake of the Aird report suited to the political realities of the time. There was to be a Canadian Radio Broadcasting Commission group of three, Hector Charlesworth, the editor of *Saturday Night* magazine, as chairman, Lt. Col. W. Arthur Steel as technical adviser and Thomas Maher, a forestry engineer was to fill the post of vice-chairman. The Commission had two main jobs; to run the radio stations and regulate Canadian broadcasting and individual broadcasters. The government retained control of the commission budget against the broadcast league's advice, but did take their advice about an increase in radio license fees and raised them from $1 to $2. Networks were to come under the commission's control and the employees of the commission were to be civil servants—a curious hodgepodge of limits which guaranteed the commission's failure. The government simply could not yet accept the idea of an independent commission modeled on the British Broadcasting Corporation.

In 1923, Hooper's equipment picked up Salvation Army band music playing below window behind him in photo. He had all sorts of requests to play it again.

It so turned out that the appointment of Hector Charlesworth as the head of the CRBC had been an unfortunate move. The CRBC had evolved because of a religious controversy and it had been hoped that its creation would end this conflict. But the opposite proved true. Charlesworth not only censored the Jehovah's Witnesses by insisting their scripts be approved by the commission before broadcasting, but they were able to prove that Charlesworth was a bigot who had described their American leader, Judge Rutherford, in his *Saturday Night* magazine, as "a heavy jowled flannelmouth." The Witnesses replied in kind by calling Charlesworth "a liar, thief, Judas and polecat, fit to associate only with the clergy." This was only the beginning of the harrassment directed towards Charlesworth and his group.

Another persistent irritant was the matter of licensing. There were no licenses required in the United States and the Canadian public resented paying a fee to listen to the radio. Laughing at the government's attempts to collect the fees became a national pastime.

But if God had been instrumental through his churches for the formation of the CRBC it was the Conservative party's advertising agency that finally destroyed it during the 1935 election campaign. Their agency, J. J. Gibbons, had created a series of dramatic political propaganda shows featuring a character known as Mr. Sage, a folksy old codger who sat on his front porch and said

25

what he thought about the Grits. The newspaper ads described Mr. Sage as "a shrewd observer who sees through the pretences, knows the facts, understands the true issues of the present political campaign and discusses the election with his friends."

Here is an excerpt from one of the scripts:

> SAGE: In 1930 . . . I happened to be staying with my brother-in-law in Quebec. . . . Mr. King's henchmen used to call up the farmers and their wives in the early hours of the morning and tell them their sons would be conscripted for war if they voted against King. . . .
>
> SAGE: He led his party down into a valley not so long ago—he himself called it the Valley of Humiliation. . . .
>
> BILL: Slush fund from Beauharnois, wasn't it?
>
> SAGE: Yes, Bill—over $700,000—and that's the man who wants to be Prime Minister of Canada. Can you beat it? . . . In the Old Country, Beauharnois would have finished him. In Canada—well, I guess people don't like that sort of thing any more than they do over there. Canadians are pretty honest folk, Bill.

The first and second broadcasts of Mr. Sage were produced September 7 and 14, 1935, starred Rupert Lucas and were broadcast on Ontario stations only, without listing the sponsor. There was so much Conservative approval of the first two dramas that it was decided that the following plays would be broadcast nationally.

The Liberals were furious and complained to Charlesworth who insisted that a sponsor be announced for the last four broadcasts but the name given as sponsor for the programs was R.L. Wright, an employee of the advertising agency, and not the Conservative party.

Although the Mr. Sage series did not manage to win the election for the Conservatives, it so infuriated Mackenzie King that he decided to reconsider the original advice of the Canadian Broadcast League and on November 2, 1936 the Canadian Broadcasting Corporation was formed.

If Mr. Sage helped bring about the CBC he also ended all future dramatizations of political broadcasts and his ghost still lingers with us. If any child should ever ask why Canadian political broadcasts are so dull a brief lecture on the six-week career of Mr. Sage should be adequate explanation.

It had taken years of bitter acrimony before the political groups realized that it would do neither party any good to have a corruptible national broadcasting system. With the formation of the CBC, a double system of private and public enterprise was created. If it did leave Canadian politicians in the role of watchdogs and critics, a role they have vigorously pursued ever since, it also set up one of the best radio systems in the world. The constant pressures between the supporters of the private and public sectors have developed the healthiest, most diversified and economic system of radio networks, stations and programs anywhere in the world.

Mackenzie King, angered by disguised Conservative political propaganda on radio, formed the CBC in 1936.

RADIO'S COPPER AGE 1906-1936
Ah, ah, ah,
...Don't Touch that Dial.

The year was 1919 and the Marconi Company in Canada which was in the radio manufacturing business decided there was only one way to develop the market — they would have to get a license to transmit programs which would interest people enough to buy radios. Simple.

The Department of Naval Services granted the company a license signed by Donald Manson, a future head of CBC, for station XWA Montreal which later became CFCF and is still broadcasting to this day. XWA was managed by A. H. Morse whose station personnel included Darby Coats and Max Smith, the man credited with the original idea of broadcasting to promote radio sales.

During 1919 this station crew had experimented to a local audience of "hams" with such stellar programs as "testing, one, two, three, etc." and in a series of articles written for the Manitoba Telephone Company about the experiments, Darby Coats reports that the decision to broadcast recorded music came about because the technicians were running out of breath repeating "one, two, three." Coats claims that the crew borrowed a record player and records from a St. Catherines Street music store in return for an "on the air" credit for the store. Canada's first radio commercial was a "contra" deal — no cash changed hands. The success of this deal apparently attracted song pluggers and piano dealers who provided the Marconi Company with free program material — a real break for station owners. They'd never have it so good again.

The first *live* talent on XWA was Gus Hill, a pop ballad singer who brought along a pianist named Willie Eckstein from the Strand Theatre also located on St. Catherine St. W. The "studio" was a bare room on the top floor of the Marconi Plant on Williams Street next door to a chocolate factory and the whole scene overlooked Griffintown, a 1919 version of low-cost housing.

A classical trio performing for CNR's stations. They were probably paid with a free weekend at a CNR hotel.

On hot days Griffintown citizens would "listen" to the radio station's programs which could be heard from the open windows of the station. There is no record of the songs performed by Mr. Hill nor are there any reviews.

There is also no mention as to whether those experiments pre-dated the official first broadcast by Miss Dorothy Lutton who sang from the studio of XWA to a distinguished audience in Ottawa. The event was a meeting of the Royal Society of Canada, the subject of the meeting, "Some Great War Inventions". Radio, not Miss Lutton, was one of the inventions and the date was May 20, 1920. The concert was reported but not reviewed by the Canadian press and present in the audience were the knowledgeable music critics W. L. Mackenzie King, Robert Borden and ViLhjalmur Stefansson. Presumably the only other listeners were the hams participating in the XWA experiment.

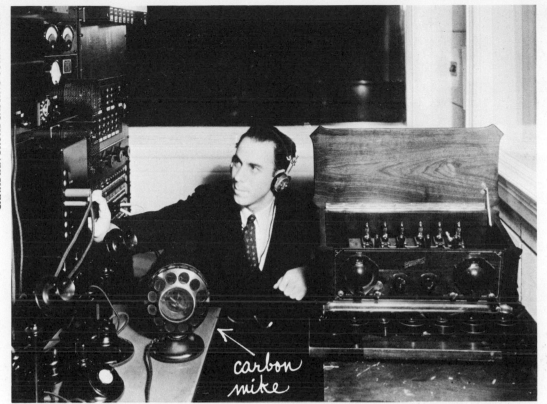

carbon mike

Arleigh Canning in CNR control room in Nova Scotia Hotel, Halifax. Ear phones were unnecessary but worn for photos to impress the public.

It's my belief, however, that credit to the first live radio singer should probably go to Mr. Hill as it seems more than likely that his radio performances took place in the summer of 1919, a year before Miss Lutton's concert.

Meanwhile the program rush was on — KDKA in Pittsburg had started up, there were broadcasts from the Hague in Holland and the Marconi Company was broadcasting daily from Chelmsford in Great Britain. By 1922 there were 39 radio licenses issued in Canada, and 91 more by 1926. At the end of 1926, however, there were only 40 still operating (the remaining 90 were not active or had gone out of business). Nine of the stations were owned by newspapers, ten by radio manufacturers and dealers, three by the CNR, one by Queens University, one by the University of Alberta and one by the Manitoba government. The others were owned by amateurs and private clubs. Most of the transmitters consisted of crude coils of wire stuck into soap boxes with switches and other devices. The receivers were crystal sets and battery-operated hetrodynes, scientific marvels that created a generation of non-sleepers who stayed up late at night to listen since that was when reception was best.

When Canadian broadcasters decided it was time to develop big radio stations in Canada they faced a real problem — the dominance of American stations that had already gobbled up most of the available radio channels

RADIO AERIAL
ON OBSERVATION CAR

LISTENING - IN
ON OBSERVATION CAR

ALL
CANADIAN
NATIONAL
RAILWAYS
Through trains, are
equipped with Radio
receiving apparatus.

TEN
Broadcasting Stations
extending Across
CANADA
FROM THE
ATLANTIC
TO THE
PACIFIC

CANADIAN NATIONAL RAILWAYS BROADCASTING STATION
AT MONCTON N.B.

BROADCASTING STUDIO
MONCTON N.B.

THE CANADIAN NATIONAL RAILWAYS
BROADCASTING STATION
OTTAWA CANADA

CNRO BROADCASTING STATION
OTTAWA ONT.

Rolly Andersen, long-distance operator on CNR train (1929). He controlled radio receivers and distributed ear phones to customers.

with their high-powered transmitters. Station licenses had been cheap and easy to obtain in the u.s. but in Canada the government had allocated only a few frequencies to each Canadian city. In Toronto for example, there were three stations owned by the newspapers, one by Eaton's, another by Bell Telephone and one each by Marconi and Westinghouse. All had to share only two broadcast frequencies which meant they had to take turns to broadcast. For each frequency there was generally one transmitter used by all of the stations, and the secondary stations in this system were generally called "shadow" or "ghost" stations.

Another problem facing Canadian stations in their competition with the Americans stemmed from the fact that up until 1925, no commercial broadcasting had been allowed in Canada. Commercials were allowed but they were credits only, simple announcements of the persons responsible for paying for the program. American radio was allowed to sell products much like present-day commercials. American domination in radio was a result of their ability to earn money while the Canadians were still content to spend it with no revenue coming in.

Since the records of the period were scratchy and of very poor quality, after the first few years broadcasters would only use "live" performers at the microphones for their programs and since no one station could afford to produce a constant stream of good programs at their own microphones broadcasters started trading their productions with other stations. This was called "chain broadcasting" with each station a link in the chain. The stations were connected with telephone lines, and one of the owners of long-distance telephone lines in Canada was the newly formed Canadian National Railway.

CNR studio orchestra arranged around microphone.

CNR broadcasting studio, Fort Garry Hotel, Winnipeg.

Moncton, New Brunswick CNR orchestra. Bell (left corner) was CNR trademark.

Typical CNR program card of the period sent out to radio fans.

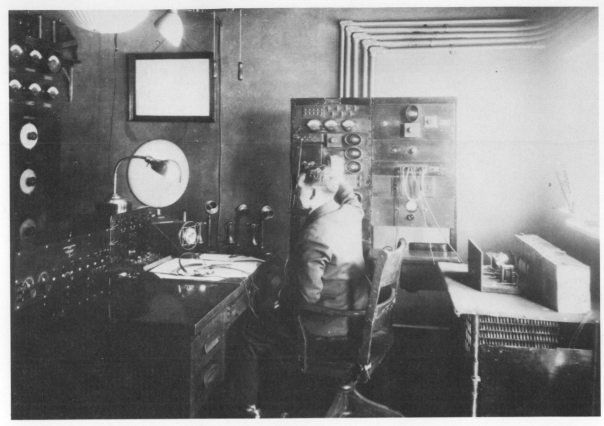

A compact CNR radio operating room in Ottawa.

CNR sound-effects photo for 1932 production of "Henry Hudson."

The Four Porters, a CNR Vancouver blackface quartet.

Cast of "Henry Hudson", first major drama of CNR's "Romance of Canada" series, produced by Tyrone Guthrie.

James McIntyre, a member of CNR orchestra.

Sir Henry Thornton, President of the CNR had decided that radios should be installed in some of the train coaches to attract new customers to the line. The next logical step was to create programs for his radios, so in 1923 he established two stations, Montreal and Ottawa, later adding a third in Moncton, N.B. By 1930 the CNR was leasing additional stations across the country in Calgary, Red Deer, Edmonton, Halifax, Strathburn, Quebec, Regina, Saskatchewan and Toronto from private stations.

Sir Henry Thornton saw the CNR railroads as a force to connect and unify Canada and its radio network as an important part of that idea. The fact that radio advertised the CNR was of course not overlooked. Sir Henry Thornton appointed Mr. J. Robb to run his network and Robb made Austin Weir program director for the CNR. Because the CNR programs were carried on private stations for only two hours a week and only one or two hours a day on the CNR's own stations the railway had to produce quality programs that

man using real phone for radio "phone effect"

C.N.R. trademark

An early CNR radio drama by Madge Macbeth (centre) in Ottawa.

would attract listeners on their trains and at home. The first big network show across Canada was the Celebration of Canada's Diamond Jubilee on July 1, 1927 broadcast by the CNR and its shadow stations. Loyal listeners at home were thrilled by the miracle of radio almost as much as the CNR passengers hurtling across the country. The program opened with a rendition of "O Canada" played on the Peace Tower's Carillon by Percival Price. A choir of 1000 children then sang appropriate songs, speeches were made by dignitaries, and Margaret Anglin, a distinguished actress of the time, read a poem written by Bliss Carman for the occasion. The Chateau Laurier orchestra played many numbers including a special suite composed by Lord Willingdon, the Hart House String Quartet was featured, the Bytown Troubadors sang folk songs and Canadian performers were featured such as Miss Eva Gauthier and Alan McQuhae. The announcers for the bilingual program were Andy Ryan and Jacques Cartier and all reports of the time indicate the show was a smashing success.

The CNR continued to produce elaborate innovative radio programs, signing the Hart House Quartet to an exclusive contract and broadcasting performances by the Toronto Symphony Orchestra. These were significant programs because listeners expected classical music. Radio was considered a "highclass" medium and only the "best" was expected to lift the tastes of the audiences. The man-on-the-street's opinion was not regarded as worthwhile, and radio was viewed mainly as a medium for the country's experts and professors.

The CNR, not content to promote only Canadian composers of classical music such as Ernest MacMillan and Clarence Lucas, also produced a fine series of dramas. Between 1927 and 1932 they produced more than 100 plays, some of them original. Most of them were produced from Vancouver to a local audience. Other performances sponsored by CNR included a cello recital by Mlle. Madeleine Monnier who was reported to have done a "novelty number", performances by a white quartet in "blackface" the Four Continental Porters from Vancouver, and a performance of Robbie Burns' poem, "The Cotters' Saturday Night". Although few of the performers who appeared on CNR radio at this time were paid they generally received free transportation, food and hotel accommodation from the CNR and this arrangement suited most of them fairly well.

Robb and Weir, the two men responsible for planning the CNR schedule, felt a genuine responsibility toward the Canadian public and always tried to come up with a balanced schedule including public services and special programs for their different audiences, even to the extent of broadcasting special pleas like the following: A Massachussets woman wrote CNRA Moncton and asked them to put a notice on radio that she was looking for a man, handsome, taller than 5 feet 8 inches, and around 175 lbs., with raven black hair, piercing eyes and a ravishing appearance. She preferred a descendant of French-Canadian settlers. Although the request was duly broadcast, history does not record whether or not she ever got her wish.

Other features on the CNR included the Dominion Observatory Time Signal which was first broadcast in March, 1924. Grain prices were reported as a service in Saskatoon in 1924, livestock prices on January 8, 1925 to Ottawa, Moncton and Winnipeg, and CNRE Edmonton covered the Farm Young People's convention in June of 1925. The Nova Scotia Provincial Exhibition at Amherst was covered as well by CNRA. Children's programs included "Bedtime Travel Tales" on CNRT, with "Uncle Alf" and Norman Cole played Uncle Dick on the children's series "Uncle Dick and Aunt Agnes".

By 1931 the CNR was satisfied it had solved most of their radio distribution problems but realized there were still problems with their programs. It was decided that the time had come to start spending money on talent. This was a new departure and the real beginning of professionalism in Canadian radio. It was Austin Weir, program director of the CNR, who convinced Mr. Robb and Sir Henry of the need for a big drama series featuring professional actors and writers. He got enthusiastic support for a projected Canadian history series titled "The Romance of Canada", travelled to England and brought back Tyrone Guthrie as producer. Merrill Denison was hired to write twenty-five scripts at $250 a script, a fee ten times larger than the going rate at that time.

The series led off with the play "The Last Voyage of Henry Hudson" which was produced after 22¹/₂ hours of rehearsal for a budget of $725. After the first year's production of sixteen plays by Guthrie, Esmé Moonie, one of radio's first woman producers, took over to complete the following season. Fortunately Merrill Denison later published several of his radio plays produced for the CNR and all of the original scripts are now in the Public Archives in Ottawa.

The CNR adventure into radio ended in 1932 for two reasons: because of the Depression the Conservative Government launched a Parliamentary investigation into the financial "excesses" of the CNR, and the Aird Commission recommended a replacement of the CNR with a nationally-owned public broadcast system. Sir Henry Thornton resigned from the CNR and the CRBC was formed to replace CNR radio. Because of Sir Henry Thornton's brilliance the CNR had developed an excellent radio system but it was the end of an era and times were changing.

BROADCASTER MAGAZINE

FOSTER HEWITT

Foster Hewitt worked in Toronto Star's roving radio station on wheels.

Typical radio transmitting building of the period.

A radio performer in the 1920s before a dual table stand with carbon mike.

And Now for a Word from....

It should be remembered, however, that the CNR was really only a small part of the radio business. The private sector was pursuing its idea separately from the network with totally different motivations — they wanted to make money, not attract passengers. Most of the experimenting in early radio, aside from the inventions discovered by the scientists, had been done by amateurs who were passionately curious about the new medium. It was therefore a natural development for these "hams" and home scientists to be among the early owners of radio stations as newspapers and electronic manufacturers, eager to be part of radio's future, instructed the zealots to get into the business. These eager beavers had to make almost all of their radio equipment from scratch — the only thing they didn't seem able to make was money.

It was not unusual at that time for many people in broadcasting to work for nothing in order to finally get credits and a paying job. The formation of the CBC did help some private radio staffers even though they had not been enthusiastic about many of the CBC's plans. For example Maritime broadcaster Syd Kennedy, never received a salary for his work at CFCY in Charlottetown until it became a CBC affiliate and he was paid from the new revenue.

While a few of the financial problems began to be solved for the staff, the need to broadcast "live" shows forced the private stations to discover talented performers who would work for nothing or next to nothing. Fortunately, classical musicians who had little outlet for their talent would perform free and club and dance musicians would appear for little money because of free publicity.

It was networking which finally provided a major source of programming. The drive towards networking had resulted because of American and Canadian laws prohibiting recordings of any kind from being broadcast in prime time between 7:30 and 11 P.M. This left stations with three choices: to produce live programs, go off the air at night or join the networks for their programs. Some private Canadian stations decided to affiliate with the CBC while others joined up with the American networks NBC, CBS or Mutual. This was possible only because there were no Canadian content laws at that time. The dabblers and amateurs had been forced out of the radio business by then and most of the private stations had their own frequencies, studio and sales staff. Sports was a natural commercial "property" and hockey was one of the earliest and most successful types of commercial broadcasts.

Hockey broadcasts started on February 8, 1923, with Norman Albert broadcasting from the Toronto arena, according to the Toronto *Globe and Mail's* sports historian, Dick Beddoes, Pete Parker is credited as the world's second hockey broadcaster while Foster Hewitt founded his hockey dynasty March 22, 1923. By 1931 the Maple Leaf Gardens had been built for the Toronto Maple Leafs and games were broadcast regularly to Montreal, and by 1933 the Saturday night games were broadcast from coast to coast on twenty stations. All of these N.H.L. broadcasts were sponsored by General Motors and provided good solid revenue for the private stations.

With or without revenue, the private stations were also experimenting with other types of complex radio productions, and western Canada proved a good breeding ground for many talented radio people. There was Mercer McLeod, a talented English actor who had begun his career as a broadcaster in Vancouver and drifted on to Trail, B.C. The CRBC contracted for a series of spooky radio dramas to be produced by McLeod for the Trail radio station. The scripts McLeod received were so bad, he ended up rewriting them, trained a local cast of actors and came up with "Ghostwalkers", one of the best radio-drama series of its time.

The private Winnipeg radio stations were also the base for men such as Tommy Tweed to produce shows like "Youngbloods of Beaver Bend." At $15 a script, Tweed also learned he would have to act as well as write for radio if he was ever going to survive. Esse Ljungh also produced shows in Winnipeg and even set up radio drama training classes, in his words "to lead the great unwashed into the promised land of radio drama."

Meanwhile in Ontario an argument and bet between a good writer and a sceptical producer resulted in Don Henshaw and producer Stanley Maxted developing "Forgotten Footsteps." Maxted bet Henshaw that he could not write an interesting radio series based on artifacts in the Royal Ontario Museum. Henshaw who had been dramatizing news turned his talents to creating exciting adventures about the people who used the items in the

A popular Canadian radio comedy in the 1930s featured Woodhouse and Hawkins.

Museum, and the results gripped a weekly radio audience for some years.

The success of this series was just another indication that audiences of the time wanted to be educated or uplifted. The programs of classical and concert music were extremely popular including "One Hour With You" a Montreal program from the Mount Royal Hotel conducted by Guiseppe Agostini, Lucio's father. The New York Philharmonic and the Metropolitan Opera broadcast from the u.s. drew large audiences as well. But people have always wanted comedy perhaps most of all and the Canadian comedy shows in the 1930s were still poor imitations of the American Amos and Andy show. When Woodhouse and Hawkins, a pair of English comics, developed their Canadian comedy show the pattern was finally broken. They started out in Calgary, moved to Winnipeg and eventually to Toronto. Their style was delightfully different from most radio comedy fare and they had a loyal audience.

Canadian country-and-western shows of the '30s were popular on radio.

Don Messer and his gang performing on radio in the '30s.

Bert Anstice and His Mountain Boys
On Tour 1935.

A series of programs which did remain imitative of the U.S. program, "The Grand Ole Opry" were the country-and-western radio shows. They included "George Wade and His Corn Huskers" from Toronto, "Bert Anstice and His Mountaineers" from Montreal and "The Singing Lumberjacks" featuring Charlie Chamberlain and the Don Messer Orchestra, from which "Don Messer and His Islanders" evolved.

But despite the attempt to produce popular Canadian programs everybody in North America was still rightly enchanted with the excellent American programs of the 1930s. The most popular programs were the Major Bowes Amateur Hour, Jack Benny, Edgar Bergen and Charlie McCarthy and Fred Allen. Listeners generally ignored Canadian shows to listen to these American stars until a Canadian tragedy grabbed the attention of radio audiences across the whole of the United States and Canada. The Moose River Mine disaster was the event and the broadcaster was J. Frank Willis.

On April 12, 1936 three men 141 feet underground in a Nova Scotia mine pulled the signal rope to bring down the "skip" and the whole mine shaft caved in on them. They were trapped. Everybody presumed these men had been killed but it appeared a few days later that maybe, just maybe, they might be alive. J. Frank Willis, the CRBC's only employee east of Montreal went to the scene of the disaster along with Arleigh Canning and Cecil Landry of CHNS as relief operator and started a marathon broadcast that had the whole of North America on tenterhooks for days. Frank Willis captured the sympathy and attention of the entire North American radio audience

Fred Allen (far left) with cast of Allen's Alley was a favorite of Canadian audiences.

Edgar Bergen and Charlie McCarthy were part of America's golden age of comedy.

J. Frank Willis, CRBC's only employee east of Montreal, proved Canadian radio ranked with the world's best with his dramatic Moose River Mine broadcasts.

Frank Willis, reporting at scene of Moose River Mine disaster, holds a desk microphone which he removed from Nova Scotia Hotel.

Frank Willis is congratulated after his marathon broadcast.

with his graphic descriptions of the rescue, and many listeners could not sleep for worrying about the trapped men. The Mayor of Winnipeg is reported to have been annoyed because the city stopped hourly to listen to Frank's reports, which were broadcast for a few minutes each hour for sixty-nine hours, until two of the three men who survived the ordeal were finally rescued. The broadcasts were carried on all 58 Canadian radio stations and 650 radio stations in the United States.

The coverage of the Moose River Mine disaster by Frank Willis was recognized as the outstanding radio news story of the first half of the twentieth century. Canadian radio had for the first time really come into its own and Canadians were now much more aware that there was a place and a need for their own kind of radio which could more than compete with the world's best.

Three years later, an event took place which was another major instance of Canadian radio admirably performing the coverage dearest to Canadian hearts — the broadcasts of the Royal Tour of 1939. Canada was fiercely loyal to King George VI and his gracious Queen Elizabeth and the lavish coverage by the CBC and its staff reflected this feeling. In fact, many old-time CBC broadcasters still date their lives from before or after that Royal Tour. The CBC spent a fortune in technical equipment necessary to cover the event — money well spent, as it so turned out, because Canada and the CBC were shortly to be faced with one of the greatest trials in their history — World War II.

51

CBC Toronto sound room staff. (Left to right) Bert Stanley with bell clanger, Fred Tudor with pistol, Gordon Tanner with soda bottle, Harold Symes with telephone effects.

The Next Sound You'll Hear....

The ultimate job in radio, the most imaginative and satisfying is that of the Sound Effects man. Who else actually gets paid money to smash glass, bark like a dog, cry like a baby and howl like a siren?

A visitor to CBC Toronto could easily mistake the sound-effects room for a junk shop but I don't believe fourteen boys let loose in an attic filled with the accumulation of a century would ever be able to create such confusion. Since 1938, junk has been accumulating on the CBC shelves without the benefits of a gentle mother's spring cleaning — old dishes, beer bottles, guitars, boxes of sand, hinges, fences, slats of wood, strips of cloth and glass — name it and it's there and the total impression is chaos.

Some of this mess sees regular service and is therefore worn by the hands of time, while a few items at the back are brand new, and have never been used, but survive under the dust for future use. Just as a prospector probes the wilderness so do our sound men probe these shelves in hope of finding the ideal sound for their show or perhaps with the lurking belief that somewhere in this confusion there may still rest a bottle of vintage wine.

All major sound rooms include "built" effects such as doors, wheels, water tanks and a glass crasher. Door frames are outfitted with various baffles to change the pitch and resonance of the sound, and the dungeon door of steel is embellished with the inevitable chains necessary for your better kind of horror shows. The sound of "Madame Guillotine" an integral part of French-revolution stories, is simulated for radio by using a sliding door and a heavy knife striking a cabbage. Another cabbage is dropped into a straw basket to complete the effect.

The Glass Crasher is everybody's favorite sound-effect instrument. Two sheets of glass are held in a twin frame, while two large brass balls on a

53

 For a single train sound effect the CNR used the following: (left to right) man with lamp, woman with bell, director cueing, announcer for "all aboard", man with "toot" whistle, man with board for "clackety-clack" sound.

pendulum smash the glass. Nothing gives more release than about ten minutes on the Glass Crasher, and nobody ever needs a psychiatrist after a work-out on that machine.

In the 1920s and early 1930s radio sound effects imitated old stage ideas about sound. At best sound effects used for the theatre stage were and still are terrible, but radio was content to use these effects for a while. The familiar sound of hoof beats made from banging coconut shells is one example. Thunder was produced by shaking large suspended sheets of steel, and buckshot rolling back and forth in cardboard tubes supposedly sounded like surf. However, in the 1930s "Atlantic Nocturne" from Halifax, experimented and successfully used several pounds of buckshot in narrow corregated troughs of wood slowly rocked from end to end for the sound of the Atlantic. The sound of marching was, and still is, produced with wooden frames holding dozens of wooden rods suspended on canvas cross-pieces rocked on the floor. Wind was simulated by covering a rotating drum of wooden slats with a sheet of canvas; for warm wind, the drum is rotated slowly, for colder winds the drum is turned faster.

thunder
sheet

bowling ball
effect

lightning
effect

wind
machine

Some Sound Devices of Radio Drama

A rare NBC photo showing a 1923 production of "Rip Van Winkle."

These ingenious effects were limited by the quality of the early micro-phones. It's hard to believe that Orson Welles in his production of "War of the Worlds" could have convinced listeners with the "reality" of his sound effects. Yet the fact remains that the effects and the script were completely convincing to a large and frightened audience. Nevertheless, sound effects have come a long way since then.

Recordings were not allowed by NBC or CBS on their broadcasts until the last years of the Second World War, and I would remind listeners who remember Ed Murrow broadcasting for CBS during a bombing raid from London that those were real bombs they heard exploding. But CBC policy was *against* dead announcers and *for* new inventions and technology. The mobile trucks used by the CBC overseas unit were in fact disc-recording studios. These recordings were later played back from the BBC to Canada. This flexibility allowed Mathew Halton, Marcel Ouimet and other Canadian

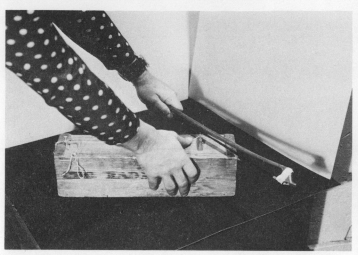

A violin bow string creates sound of squeaky door.

Old audio tape squeezed makes sounds of footsteps in grass.

correspondents to get to the scenes of action and return with the actual sounds of war on records. During the war Art Holmes, one of the CBC technicians, recorded the raids over London for several nights. Many of these records are now in the BBC Sound Effects Library and remain the best collection of bombing sound effects available on record.

After the Second World War, sound-effect companies did a major business selling recorded sounds to radio stations, networks and theatres for productions. In most cases these libraries were excellent and a few still operate in the industry. The best known libraries included Major, Standard, Gennet, Silver Masque, BBC and Speedy Q which spreads grooves at certain places on their records so the operator could visually see where to put the pickup needle for a change in the effect.

Sound-effect recordings need special equipment for playback. Playback units have several turntables with two playback arms available to each table, and the turntables have variable speed controls ranging from very slow to

Machine for sound of wagon wheels.

Slapstick for sound of gun shots.

Pay phone sound.

Machine for sound of creaking ropes on ships.

very fast. These contraptions come in various shapes and sizes but they are always called "Cocktail Bars". Unlike the old phonographs, sound-effects pickup arms have vertical styli, so they can be played on a record whether it's "coming" or "going". This allows a pickup arm between two tables to be used on either table. When a long continuous recorded effect is required, such as the hum of a motor car, a single disc is used but the pickup arms are alternated to provide a continuous sound.

Better microphones and amplifiers have changed sound techniques. For example, thunder sheets were replaced with rubber bladders from soccer balls containing a few pieces of buckshot. If snapped the right way beside a microphone, a convincing thunderclap is heard on the air. Thunder then graduated to a "thunder screen" which is a two-foot wooden square frame with stretched copper fly screen attached. Soldered to one corner of the screen is a small pin which is inserted into a record playback head. Striking the wire with a drum stick creates a tremendous storm. Thunder has always

Iron bar striking anvil for blacksmith shop effects.   *Glass Crasher machine.*

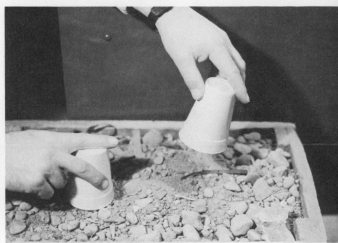

Coconut shells on gravel simulate a horse trotting.   Styrofoam cups on gravel simulate a horse "tiptoeing".

been one of the favorite sounds of radio, and no other effect had so much work lavished on its development, perhaps because we still think of it as the voice greater than ourselves.

Guns and cannons have had almost as much work lavished on them. Real guns with blanks were used for years but they were a bother. They really were not reliable and there are many stories told of guns failing to fire. Often an actor would say, "O.K. I'm going to shoot you," — a long silence — "O.K. I'll stab you then," the actor would frantically improvise — silence and then "Bang!"

Blanks also make too loud a sound and are hard on the actors and the microphones. For years the best gun effects were simulated by "slap sticks", pieces of wood slapped together, and sometimes a hardwood "yard stick" was used for gun shots. This effect is reliable so long as the slap stick does not break or crack. The ricochet of a bullet was reproduced orally, but now it is usually reproduced electronically and occasionally recorded. The trouble

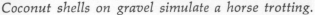

Plastic mold on glass for sound of screeching tires.   Jail door effect.

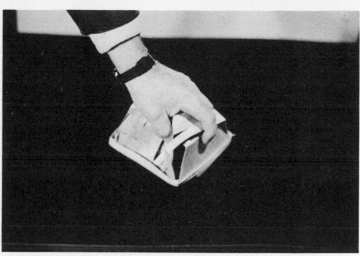

Squeezing cornstarch boxes creates sound of man walking through snow.

Crushing a berry box creates sound of tree falling.

with "slap sticks" was that an army of sound men were needed to reproduce one gun battle. There is now an electronic "Gun Shot Generator" that can do single shots, with or without ricochets, through to heavy cannon, machine guns, pom poms — in fact, a complete war by merely pushing buttons. Sounds great! As microphones improved, crumpled cellophane was used for the sound of fire and cornstarch boxes appropriately squeezed sounded like footsteps in the snow. A crushed one-quart berry box successfully simulated falling trees.

Some actual recorded sounds never do sound right on radio. For example, traffic sounds in a downtown area require studio recreation with records of quiet traffic, a few voices and the odd car horn. Voices cannot be heard over the sound of real vacuum cleaners and sewing machines seldom sound like sewing machines to radio listeners. Often the sound man rigs the sound by using effects that sound like what the listener expects to hear. Cold wind is pitched higher than warm wind because the listener thinks that's the way it

"Harvey" is used when a body is thumped or bumped.   *Army marching sound effect.*

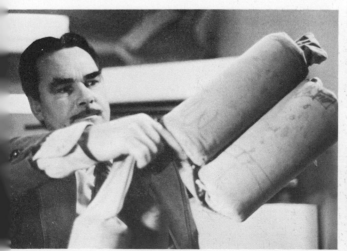

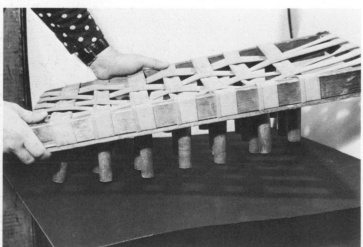

Dave Tasker (with pipe) slamming door for drama starring Joy LaFleur, John Drainie, and Bud Knapp.

is. It isn't. But in most cases the best sound effects are captured by using actual sounds of the real thing.

One ingenious creation of sound I've encountered was dreamed up by John Sliz who is now the Chief Sound Man at CBC Toronto. For the sound of a heart beating he uses a large new telephone book which he holds in his hands, the book suspended so that the bottom corners of the pages are loose. He then flaps the pages gently together in such a way that they sound exactly like the beating of a human heart.

Certain sound sequences are made up of combinations of recorded, live and rigged effects. The sound of wooden sailing ships would be created by using a combination of recorded wind and waves, live water splashes, recorded gulls, live and recorded rigging creaks, and live, recorded and rigged groaning of the timbers as the ship rides the waves.

While I have nothing but praise for the Canadian sound-effects men, I must take off my hat to that crazy breed of sound men developed in the u.s. Because of the restrictions on recordings at NBC and CBS, most of those marvellous sounds used during the American Golden Age of Radio were done with elaborate and expensive equipment or by vocal imitation. In Hollywood one

door

"Opportunity Knocks" provided little sound work for Bert Stanley (behind door) who opened show with "knock, knock" and that was it.

whole wall of a studio was required to do train sound effects until sound men started to imitate trains, planes and other sounds with their mouths and tongues. The most famous sound man was Mel Blanc who became a legend as the voice of Bugs Bunny and other cartoon characters in the movies. As Jack Benny's sound man, Mel Blanc was responsible for Benny's Maxwell, and managed to create a complete character for the car.

In New York there were two famous men who could do almost any sound orally. Brad Barker did "big sounds" like planes, trains and large animals including the lion for the MGM trademark, and the rooster on Pathe's news. Don Bain specialized in "small sounds" like birds, and smaller animals and was particularly prized for his ability to create sounds for black widow spiders and other tiny horrors.

The NBC sound-effects department was originally run by a Canadian, Ted Slade, who created sound for the radio dramas in Toronto in the early 1930s. In 1945 the NBC and the ABC sound-effects department were one and the same, and they went in more for elaborate "group" effects. An 8-by-6-foot sound-

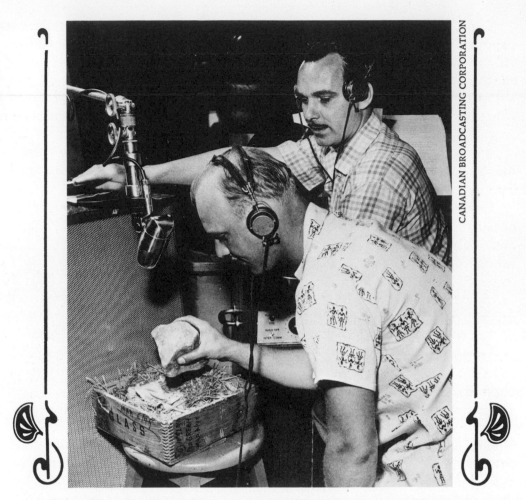

CANADIAN BROADCASTING CORPORATION

John Sliz with rock creating sound for Alex Sheridan to record for CBC.

effect truck had all possible combinations of train sounds and there was another truck used just for the sounds of fire engines. American sound men are members of the actors unions, AGFA or AFTRA, and radio actors are not allowed to make any sound effects other than crowd sounds or their assigned speaking parts.

American networks have traditionally produced action series and therefore their attitude and use of sound differed from Canadian networks who had to develop effects for the more gentle anthology series that we tend to produce. If you judged American homes by radio drama it would appear that no rooms ever had rugs on the floor and doors are always kept shut. On the American soap-operas, some shows seemed to consist of nothing but the continuous sounds of people walking in and out of doors, accompanied by actors wearing hard-soled shoes. The gumshoe never had a chance in U.S. radio.

Canadian producers used sound quite differently. For example, Rupert Caplan always felt that sound effects interfered with the words and used them only where it was essential to the plot. Andrew Allan also distrusted sound-effects men though he had the best available, and Lister Sinclair as a radio writer concurred with Allen. Andrew used sound only where he had to, and when he used it, used it brilliantly. Sometimes in a complex scene he would break a sound sequence into individual elements and then direct them slowly cue by cue so that the listener knew exactly what was happening. I was always convinced that these sequences were too slow to follow, but I never met a listener who agreed with me.

Esse Ljungh was also a master at using sound effects and live actors, and his production of "1984" was a sound epic. However, Esse did like to minimize "drone effects" such as airplanes or car interiors. He would state the sound at the beginning of a scene and add it here and there throughout the scene. Since Esse had been a sound-effects man in Winnipeg in the 1930s, he was extremely fussy about important effects, and he encouraged the sound department to use their imagination as much as possible.

Frank Willis adored sound effects, and he proclaimed Freddie Tudor the greatest living sound man in the business. Frank liked lots of sound and he liked it loud, and he was in heaven when he produced historical extravaganzas. Sometimes on an Esse Ljungh or Andrew Allan production there was some doubt for a few seconds as to the location of the scene if a listener had just tuned in. Never with a Frank Willis production. On his series "Great Days of Sail," Willis used as many as four sound men because he insisted that each ship must have an uniquely identifiable sound for the listeners. How those ships creaked, groaned and rolled and pitched! And how the actors loved the series: "Aloft you" — "mind the lightning" (roar of thunder) "all hands man the sails" (sound of feet running) "quickly man, reef the sails, or old Davy Jones will have guests this terrible night" (a loud crack) "She's falling. Clear the decks" (crash, scream, crackle of fire) "Quick men, the fire hoses. Run my boys." (rumble of thunder) "Curse you storm."

Generally, however, Canadian sound effects were more often used for the "sounds of silence" and records were used more often than in the u.s. For example, on the "Jake and the Kid" series, listeners would hear the call of a loon on a Northern lake or the distant sound of a locomotive as the Kid lay in bed daydreaming. Music, of course, was always a vital part of radio sound effects and Canadian composers and conductors have always been masters when it came to integrating sound effects and music.

The Toronto cbc sound-effect department was started in 1938 by Harold Symes and a year later expanded with Bert Stanley, Bill McKlintock and Gord Tanner. Freddie Tudor joined them a little later, and this remained the basic group throughout the war years. Each man had specific talents and skills. One

BROADCASTER MAGAZINE

In a contemporary sound dubbing room John Sliz watches Al Rosen feed video tape onto monitor.

man would be an expert playing records, another on bird effects, a third a whiz using a rubber-bladed electric fan for dog fights and other air battles. Bert Stanley was an excellent all-round sound man. He was also a hemophiliac, and when during a glass-crashing sequence on a drama, the glass failed to crash, Bert smashed it with his fist. Bert risked a week in hospital for a sound effect. He was typcial of sound men. They're nuts.

Although it was rare, soundmen could and did make mistakes, as happened when Bill Strange was producing, directing and acting in a sea story on the "Fighting Navy" series. When a helpless unarmed Canadian ship was stopped by a surfaced enemy sub the brave commander (Bill Strange) described to his crew the deadly events including "They've got their forward gun uncovered. Ah yes, there's a puff of smoke. In a brief moment we will hear the sound of their gun since sound travels slower than light. I can hear it now." *RRR, RRR,* came the sound of an old automobile starting. Strange looked to heaven for understanding and stomped out of the live broadcast leaving John Drainie to take over his part on the show.

I once produced a dreadful series of children's programs called "Billy Bartlett of the Double Bar U." This was one of CBC's attempts to use radio drama to show how romantic the Canadian West really was. The series was a bore, and so dull that the sound men gathered around to help me. I can recall having as many as five sound men on the set, even though only two were assigned. While the actors valiantly droned on the careful listener could hear first the call of a crow "caw, caw", then — a gunshot — "blam!", then a pitiful "caw, caw" as a crow supposedly hit the dust. Near the end of the series things had gotten so far out of control that there was the sound of cannons shooting at the crows, calves being born, and cows being serviced, and I had to call a halt. I realized that if the sound men had their way the show would have consisted of nothing but the sounds of crossfire as every songbird in Canada hit the dust.

These sound sequences were very "in" for a small group of fans, including Alan McFee. He thoroughly enjoyed this show, and contributed secretly from the network booth. Alan's nickname is "Blackie" and so was Billy Bartlett's horse. The show always opened with Billy Bartlett shouting "Blackie" (Blackie whinnies in the distance) "Come on Blackie" (whinnies again) "That's a boy, come on Blackie" (whinny, sound of hooves running, and music, as the horse approaches). One time when the author Alf Harris, played back the show's tapes to his horror he heard the following: Billy shouting "Blackie", and a voice replying, "Yes?" "Come on Blackie." "I'm here, stupid." This program was broadcast to youngsters all across Canada and the author was understandably furious. I suspected McFee but when he was accused, he denied any involvement, swore loyalty to the show, and even went so far as to accuse the furious Harris of rigging his own tape.

Bill Roach was also a master of live sound effects and could imitate many machines and some animals. His best/worst sounds were dog barks. In the halls of the CBC Bill would trail an unsuspecting victim, at the right moment pinching the victim's Achilles tendon and barking. This was funny only to the onlookers, and when Bill's trick became well-known many people swore that they would punch him out if he ever did it to them. None of them ever recovered from the first shock fast enough to get him though. I know — I was one of his victims.

I am pleased to report that we finally had our revenge on Bill. One Sunday morning Bill Roach was working on a program with Jackie Rae, a glamorous producer who later became a television star in Canada and the U.K. Jackie had brought his two beautiful boxer dogs to work with him that day. Bill was in the sound-effects room, which was at the end of the studio hall, carefully pouring corn starch from one bag to another because a snow-walking effect was required. As Bill was performing this delicate operation he was unaware that one of Jackie's dogs had walked up behind him. The dog barked — Bill and the corn starch rose three feet in the air — he landed covered in corn starch and shame, as the onlookers applauded vengefully.

The Hudson's Bay Company presents the "rent" to King George VI during the 1939 Royal Tour.

RADIO'S SILVER AGE 1936-1949
Radio Rallies
Round the Flag

The Second World War plunged Canadians into a whole new era, and for Canadian radio it was also the beginning of a new age with a different set of problems and challenges. In 1939 the United States had not yet come into the war, and unbelievable as it may seem, the CBC had not yet developed its own news service. For the first time in its history Canadian radio was now forced to produce its own original programming rather than imitations of American programs, to suit its war-time needs.

One of the most important broadcasts before the war was the Royal Tour of May, 1939. Mackenzie King was anxious that the CBC do an excellent job covering the tour and it was decided that 100 members of its small staff would be used. Ernie Bushnell co-ordinated the efforts of the thirteen announcers, while Steve Brodie set up a school to teach CBC staff the protocol of Royal Tours. Two broadcast teams leap-frogged the country — one team led by Bob Bowman and the other by T.O. Wiklund. The announcers included Ted Briggs, Fernand LeClerc, H. Rooney Pelletier, Gerry Wilmot, Bill O'Reilly, Jack Peach, Reid Forsee, Patrick Freeman, Bud Walker, Bob Anderson and John Kannawin. The French team included Jacques DesBaillets, L. Francouer and Gerry Arthur. There was a special trooping of the colour commentator, G. A. Browne and Frank Willis came back from Australia to join the crew.

This remarkable troop spent six weeks in continuous travel crossing 7000 miles to cover the tour. They produced 91 broadcasts and in the process became the heroes of the CBC. But one of the major benefits of the Royal Tour which could not be foreseen was that when it was over the CBC owned enough technical equipment to survive the following years of war.

67

Until the war there had been no real demand for a CBC news service because the newspapers had functioned well enough for peacetime. But with the U.S. at peace and Canada at war, Canadians were now anxious for the news that was relevant to them. Although the Canadian Press news service could have been available to radio broadcasters before the war, the radio industry had generally preferred highly coloured and dramatic news stories which were more entertainment than news and neither fair nor accurate according to qualified newsmen. When the war made it evident that there was a real need for Canadian Press news services they gave the news to the CBC free in order to prevent radio news from going "commercial." This stopped the commercialization of Canadian radio news for years.

In 1940 Dan McArthur was appointed to head CBC news and establish a reliable and accurate news service. Four regional news bureaus were established at Halifax, Montreal, Winnipeg and Vancouver and a central newsroom was created in Toronto. Here are three of the set of ten news directives which reflected the society of the time: no suicides were to be reported unless the people concerned were prominent, physical handicaps or deformities were to be avoided and no stories about lotteries or gambling odds for sports events were to be mentioned.

The main bulletins were broadcast morning, noon, supper and late evening. Two were national and two regional—the nationals were at noon and 11 P.M. eastern time. The 11 P.M. broadcast became known in the CBC as "The National" a term still used on the late-night major newscast on television. The BBC news was also broadcast twice a day and a half-hour BBC newsreel in the evening.

The first regular news reader on the CRBC and later the CBC was Charles Jennings. He was followed by Lorne Greene who became famous as "The Voice of Doom" during the war. Later, near the end of the war, Earl Cameron took over for ten years to be succeeded by Harry Mannis, Bill Read and Frank Herbert.

During the war the government asked the CBC to move The National from 11 to 10 P.M. eastern time so people would go to bed earlier and save power and fuel for the war effort. Because of this it became a fixed habit for most Canadians to listen to Lorne Greene read the news and then trot off to bed. The CBC broadcasts were available to all Canadian radio stations regardless of affiliation. Many stations took the national and regional newcasts because the censorship regulations were so complex that it was safer to let the CBC worry about censorable national news and continue to use only local and "safe" news from their own newsrooms. Even local news was rigidly controlled however, and certain types of news were classified in parts of Canada at that time, including weather forecasts, transportation information, crop reports and even on occasion, news of disasters.

Lorne Greene was known as the "Voice of Doom" during World War II. Inserts show Greene fighting fatigue during a broadcast.

▲ CBC war correspondent Benoit LaFleur recording at Italian front.

Marcel Ouimet, CBC correspondent at the front. ▲

▼ CBC engineer Arthur Holmes shows the CBC mobile recording van he operated in World War II campaigns to George Drew, Premier of Ontario.

CBC engineer Harold Wadsworth just prior to taking off in a bomber to record impressions over enemy territory.

Among the special news services provided by the CBC during the war was the broadcasting of Canadian news overseas through the facilities of the BBC. The news was cabled from the CBC central newsroom for a weekly 15-minute broadcast read by Byng Whitteker as well as 10-minute sportscasts the following day which would include the hockey scores for Canadian soldiers. In Canada the CBC broadcast a similar service to Australians and New Zealanders.

The CBC overseas news unit did a magnificent job, described by Bert Powley in his own book *A Broadcast From The Front* which tells of the trials and tribulations of the Canadian news correspondents during the war. As well as feeding the regular newscasts the overseas unit also produced program material for two or more broadcasts weekly. "With the Troops" was broadcast in England on Mondays and "English Newsletter to Canada" covered the activities of Canadian men and women overseas on Thursdays. Bob Bowman was head of these units and Art Holmes was the first technician.

The CBC war correspondents made quite a name for themselves — especially Mathew Halton and Marcel Ouimet for the French, as well as Peter Stursburg and Benoit LaFleur who both covered the news in Italy. Other overseas war correspondents were J. L. Beauregard, Andrew Cowan, Bill Herbert, Paul Barette, Alex MacDonald, Lloyd Moore, Cliff Spear, Fred McCord, Paul

CBC war correspondents Benoit LaFleur (left) and J. L. Beauregard recording Canadian army news in Italy.

Johnson, Bert Powley, Harold "Waddy" Wadsworth, Claude Dostie, John Kannawin and newsmen like Greg Clark. It was because of these men's efforts that in 1943 CBC won the most prestigious award possible, the Ohio Award for news coverage.

While the news correspondents played a vital and brave part of wartime broadcasting, in my opinion the wartime commentators played just as important a part at that crucial time. They were able to bring a much-needed focus to war events because they operated independently of government and propaganda controls, using the "man on the street's" information and relating it to their own hunches and experience. While the authorities considered propaganda necessary for wartime morale, the calm reasoning of these perceptive men allowed the listeners to have a true overview of what was really happening overseas.

The commentators were an interesting selection of experts — from the U.K. men like J.B. Priestly and J.B. (Hamish) McGeachy, from New York Raymond Gram Swing who alternated with James M. (Don) Minifie from Washington. Willson Woodside was another Toronto expert who did commentaries on war strategy.

Winston Churchill's motto — "Give us the tools and we will finish the

Viscount Alexander of Tunis examines CBC truck which was actually a small radio studio on wheels.

job"—governed a large part of the Canadian radio war effort. But tools cost money so early in the war the sale of War Savings Bonds and Victory Bonds was the focus for a series of broadcasts. Often, the top Canadian news correspondents were dragged back from England to take part in these events much to their frustration. In 1941 all sorts of American stars came up to Canada to participate—Percy Faith who had left the CBC for the u.s., Andre Kostelanetz, Paul Whiteman, Bob Hope, John Charles Thomas, Gracie Fields, Morton Downey, Arch Oboler, Irving Berlin, and Ronald Coleman all contributed to Canadian War Bonds broadcasts. The programs were generally musicals with "pitches" by the stars, which sometimes included very effective dramatic sketches describing the heroic efforts taking place to win the war.

A number of radio series were also produced to spur Canadian audiences on to win the war. The series "Arsenal of Democracy" described the development of new industries needed for the war effort. "Carry on Canada" "Talks about Tanks" "Steel Production" and "Guns and Ammunition" were other shows of that period.

British Ballad Operas were also produced to inspire Canadians to appreciate the courage and humor of the British. Scheduled on the National network, in effect the programs consisted of British music for British listeners. Operas produced under the supervision of Jean Marie Beaudet included, "Hugh the Drover" by Vaughan Williams, "Merrie England" by Edward German and Balfe's "Bohemian Girl." Canadian conductors were Ernest MacMillan, and Eugene Goossens and singers included Rose Bampton and John Brownlee of

73

Canadian radio rallied round the flag with Winston Churchill's motto as focus.

Radio sing-songs were an important way to raise money for War Savings Bonds.

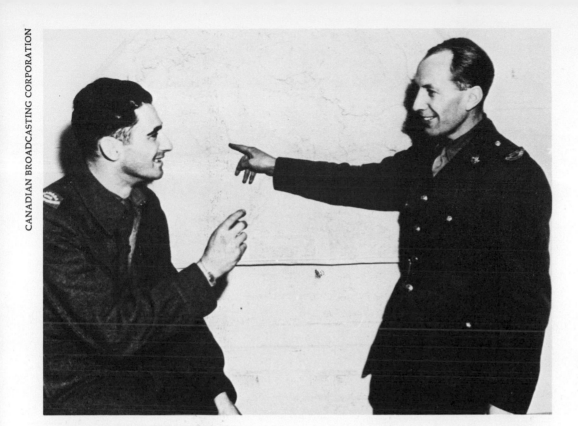

Peter Stursberg (left) and Matthew Halton, one of the most respected Canadian war correspondents.

the New York Metropolitan Opera along with many Canadian singers. John Coulter and Healey Willan wrote a Canadian "Odyssey of 1942" entitled "Transit Through Fire" which concluded the British series with an all-Canadian cast. Nationalism was beginning to develop in Canada but the concept of "Canadian content" as a percentage of broadcasting was not even considered at this time. Coulter recalls being paid less than $500 for the rental of the libretto by the CBC. He thinks the fee was $350 — an incredibly low fee for such an outstanding playwright. The CBC blurb for this series reflects the attitude of the times as they describe the programs "bringing to listeners knowledge of an essential element in Britain's genius, hence these programs mark a definite musical contribution to national morale, and to the spiritual side of our war effort."

It was however the dramas of the time that remain the best-remembered wartime programs. At first the BBC sent over script and transcriptions for broadcast in Canada. These programs were written to help clarify the war situation for Canadian listeners and included shows like "Under the Shadow of the Swastika" and "A Half-Hour with Mr. Jones."

The most outstanding Canadian series was "Theatre of Freedom" broadcast Sunday nights during the spring of 1941, produced by Rupert Lucas with the help of two American producers. According to the CBC blurb "These per-

75

Vancouver wartime radio drama with actors dressed up for publicity photo later used as propaganda.

formances were an offering made by our playwrights and actors to the cause of democracy, which is at stake in the World War today. The stars of Hollywood and Broadway, the dramatists of the stage, film and radio, gave freely of their best to Canada, as a means of heartening and inspiring the listening audience throughout the Dominion and beyond its borders."

The main Canadian effort in wartime drama was a development of "Carry on Canada" which became a weekly drama series produced on a rotating basis on behalf of the three military services, under the title, "Comrades in Arms." Frank Willis was the producer and Samuel Hersenhoren led the orchestra. These musical productions with dramatic sketches survived long after the war and ran as late as 1950. The original writers "reported" on behalf of their respective services—Bill Strange wrote for the navy, Dick Diespecker for the Army and A.A. McDermott with Fletcher Markle for the Air Force.

Frank Shuster (left) and Johnny Wayne (centre) with army show in France.

Johnny Wayne and Frank Shuster in a publicity shot to promote sale of war bonds.

By 1950 the program was produced by Jackie Rae with Howard Cable conducting and Leslie Bell leading the choir. Singers included were Gisele Lafleche, Terry Dale and Ted Hockridge. John Rae (no relation to Jackie Rae) was the announcer and Larry McCance was the man in uniform. Bill Strange was still writing for the Navy, George Salverson was writing for the Army and Max Braithwaite for the R.C.A.F. and the service rivalry lasted up to the end of the series.

Bill Strange (who later became the General Manager of the Jamaica Broadcasting Corporation) became the driving force behind "Fighting Navy" one of the most successful war series produced. A "heroes" series, the scripts were based on "true adventures" which took place on a mythical destroyer H.M.C.S. Missinabi under the command of "The Captain" played by Mercer McLeod. Lloyd Bochner played the young sailor Jack Marlowe, and he was replaced by Vincent Tovell when Lloyd joined the real navy. The cast of Fighting Navy became a "who's who" of great radio actors after the war, including John Drainie, Austin Willis, Howard Milsom, Jack Fuller, Lister Sinclair, Peggi

Big bands such as Mart Kenney's orchestra were an integral part of radio in the '40s.

Loder, Francis Goffman and Pauline Rennie. Iris Alden was the director of the series and B.A. Oil sponsored the program which was broadcast on Thursday nights.

Air Force fans also had their own wartime show, a drama "L for Lanky", sponsored by the Canadian Marconi Company, written by Don Bassett, and produced by Alan Savage. Again true war stories were implanted on a fictional bomber "L for Lanky". This show was almost as successful as "Fighting Navy" and included in the cast were Jack Fuller, Jules Upton, George Murray (the tenor), Herb Gott, Art Martin and Vincent Tovell.

The army and the merchant navy also had shows dedicated to their special audiences—the "Merchant Navy Show" had Corby MacNeil as M.C. with Howard Higgins' orchestra and the program consisted primarily of music. Shuster and Wayne, and Russ Titus were stars of the Army Show, which was actually a touring variety stage show that was broadcast occasionally. After the war John and Frank went on to do the "Johnny Home" show which dealt with the problems of repatriation.

Virginia Payne
(Ma)

Murray forbes

Charles
Egelston

"Ma Perkins", one of the weepiest American soap operas of the '40s had many loyal Canadian fans.

To round out the war effort there were also many religious programs and services, and inspirational programs of music and writing. Alistar Grosart and John Weinzweig combined to produce "New Canadians", a series about people who had fled Europe. Margaret Kennedy and Anne Mariott wrote a verse program "Who's Johnny Canuck?" Harry Red Foster contributed a verse play "British Birthright" about freedom and Gerald Noxon wrote a series of fourteen programs titled "They Fly for Freedom" which was recruiting propaganda for the R.C.A.F.

But the CBC didn't have a corner on patriotism and the private sector of radio and sponsors were responsible for many programs including morale-building singsongs in the parks and, of course, the big network commercial programs.

"Command Performance" was one of the outstanding commercial series combining music with a dramatic sketch about war heroes. The program had a generous budget supplied by Supertest Gasoline, and Harry Foster organized the series and wrote a special tribute to war heroes which was read by Lorne

Greene. In 1944 the heroes honoured were all Victoria Cross winners. Much of the special music was composed by Lucio Agostini, with Sir Ernest MacMillan conducting and the program was produced at the concert studio of the CBC.

A similar program of that period was "Borden's Canadian Cavalcade" again with Lorne Greene narrating a story about a war hero. The program featured popular songs as well, with announcer Cy Mack and music conducted by Howard Cable. Rai Purdy produced the series through Young and Rubicam, a major advertising agency. The show was a chatty affair with Cy Mack talking to the singers, special guests and the weekly hero. A narrative set the scene to introduce a guest who had seldom been on radio before, but because of censorship the ad libs were written beforehand. One interview was with a manufacturer of a submarine detection device whose employees did not know what they were actually making. (From the script it appears that they were improving Fessenden's submarine inventions.) The commercials sold Klim and ended with the motto "If it's Borden's it's got to be good."

Even the soap-operas revolved around the war and "Soldier's Wife" written by Kay and Ernie Edge, featured a character, Carry Murdock with a husband George stationed overseas as a sergeant in the Hullyvale Rifles. The program sponsored by the Wartime Prices and Trade Board, carried a lot of propaganda for the listeners, and the commercials supplied useful data to housewives concerning ration regulations and other important information. This was one of the few "soaps" that both entertained and served a purpose. "John and Judy" was yet another domestic drama in which the characters, a delightful couple played by Bill Needles and Roxanna Bond, had to cope with situations dealing with problems caused by wartime regulations.

It must be obvious to readers by now that the war did indeed change radio broadcasting in Canada. Now for the first time in their history Canadians were listening to a lot of original Canadian programs. This had happened not only because of the war but because the CBC had made a conscious decision to control the number of war broadcasts and maintain a reasonable balance between entertainment programs and the stark brutal facts of the war brought to listeners by the news and public affairs broadcasts. Some of the best and funniest American radio programs of all time were carried now on the CBC network as well as some of the weepiest American soap operas such as Ma Perkins, The Man That I Married, and The Right to Happiness, daily features which enthralled the housewives. Evening features included Lux Radio Theatre, The Voice of Firestone, Carnation Contented Hour, Fibber McGee and Molly and Jack Benny. With good original Canadian programs and top shows from the United States, Canadians were receiving the best of both radio worlds and they were enjoying it. Radio had become an integral part of their lives.

The early years of the CBC had been spent consolidating program distribu-

American radio comedy was in its heyday during the '40s and Fibber McGee and Molly were beloved by Canadian listeners.

tion, expanding existing programs and improving program areas which had been neglected. During Canadian radio's Silver Age which lasted from the mid-1930s to the mid-1940s, schools, farm and women's broadcasts were also established. Until this time these features had been represented only in the most casual way, but now they became an important part of radio.

Farm broadcasting, a major development in the CBC began on French-Canadian radio April 11, 1938. The program was called "Le Reveil Rural". The

Peter Whittal Gordon Howard Grace Webster Frank Peddie Alice Hill

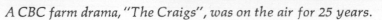

A CBC farm drama, "The Craigs", was on the air for 25 years.

English language service followed February 29, 1939. Radio was to play a big part in helping the Canadian farmer improve his lot and his production. Prior to this there had been some stock market reports from Winnipeg and Toronto and the Alberta commercial network had carried some farm news. But CBC broadcasts were to become more than news—they were a propaganda platform to help convince the farmer that good farming led to good living. Orville Shugg was hired by Ernie Bushnell to broadcast fifteen minutes a day for three months, at $50 a broadcast. He stayed for five years. The new program was so successful that later Shugg added "The Craigs" a farm drama written by Dean Hughes that lasted for 6,138 programs for twenty-five years, ending July 31, 1964. Shugg initiated regional broadcasts in the Maritimes and the Prairies in 1939 and in British Columbia in 1940.

The farm dramas were a vital part of the farm broadcasts and each region had its own. In Winnipeg "The Jacksons" and in the Maritimes "The Gillans" were the farming family and in B.C. it was "The Carsons". The "Carsons" also ran for twenty-five years and 6,022 scripts were written, most of them by David Savage. The broadcasting of dramatized propaganda was extremely

CANADIAN BROADCASTING CORPORATION

The Blattnerphone, the earliest tape recorder, used high-quality steel for tape but war-time shortage of steel prohibited its use.

successful; effective for the farmer and lucrative for a distinguished group of Canadian actors. The authors, unfortunately, were never paid as much as they deserved. A lot of outstanding radio people worked on those broadcasts and it was finally rumoured that the only way to achieve a senior position in the CBC was to become a farm broadcaster. For example, Ron Fraser became a vice-president and farm broadcasters, Keith Morrow and Bob Graham became senior program executives. The current czar of radio and television English programming is ex-farm commentator Norn Garriock and the vice-president of the CRTC is former farmer Harry Boyle. Farm commentator Neil Morrison became the head of the CBC talks department during the 1950s and another, Fergus Mutrie, became a senior TV executive. Even Orville Shugg who left after five years with the farm broadcasts returned years later to a senior position in CBC Sales Policy. Is there substance to the rumor? I leave it to the reader.

If CBC executives came out of farm broadcasts, so did some of Canada's finest radio writers, actors and producers. Up until the mid-1930s Canada hadn't given a damn about Canadian talent. The worst imports were paid

Wishart Campbell

Andrew Allan

It wasn't until the 1940s that Canadian dramatists like Andrew Allan were given a chance on CBC radio.

much more than Canadians and foreign experts received higher fees and more prestige despite the superior talent languishing in our own country. In drama for instance, only token efforts had been made to develop Canadian writers and in the world of Canadian drama, actors and producers had been frustrated at not being able to get on "their" air. In the u.s. drama was already a big part of the radio scene, but the CBC was too busy consolidating its positions to care about the fact that acting colonies across Canada were "doing their own thing" on private radio. Winnipeg, for example, had two active "theatre stations" CKY owned by the Manitoba Telephone Company and CKNC owned by James Richardson. Tommy Tweed and Esse Ljungh, along with many others, cut their dramatic teeth with little or no pay on these stations. In Vancouver, Fletcher Markle, John Drainie and Alan Young were learning their craft while in Toronto. Andrew Allan, Bob Christie and Rai Purdy produced CFRB material. The institution of the Farm Broadcasts finally supplied a professional base for Canadian actors. Rupert Lucas was made head of the CBC drama department and his job was to fan this creativity and harness the existing talent.

The cast of "One Man's Family", a soap opera that brought tears to the eyes of listeners and dollars to the pockets of sponsors.

Things began to happen for Canadian writers too. Ironized Yeast sponsored a program "Canadian Theatre of the Air" which had planned to use imported scripts for Canadian actors, but as the series developed it became apparent to the producers that there were Canadians who could write good scripts. The producers changed their buying pattern and as a result 47 of the 65 scripts were written by Canadians. Yes, Canadian radio dramatists were finally gaining recognition but meanwhile the CBC found itself once more embroiled in the kind of dramatic episode they feared most — religious controversies, sparked off by radio broadcasts had once more provided a country-wide stage for both ministers and politicians.

In the CBC files are hundreds of documents concerning the two separate incidents that bruised the CBC like never before or since. The first incident concerned a Presbyterian minister, Morris Zeidman who had presented some very strong views about the Catholic Church and birth control on a CFRB radio program in Toronto. As the regulatory body, the CBC felt obliged to inform Mister Zeidman that he was not allowed to use radio in this way. That did it! The two Toronto daily newspapers took opposite stances about the program and Toronto's Orangemen rose up to defend Zeidman. The CBC was accused of censorship and worse, censoring loyal Britishers in this freedom-loving Dominion. The following telegram from Zeidman to the Prime Minister gives some indication of the furor:

TORONTO ONT JAN 10 1937
THE RIGHT HON W L MACKENZIE KING
PRIME MINISTER OF CANADA OTTAWA ONT.
ON BEHALF OF THE HUNDREDS OF THOUSANDS OF LISTENERS-IN TO THE PROTESTANT RADIO LEAGUE STUDY HOUR WE WISH TO EXPRESS OUR DEEP INDIGNATION AT THE DECISION OF THE CAN. BROADCASTING COMMISSION HINDERING THE PREACHING OF NEW TESTAMENT CHRISTIANITY OVER THE AIR IN THE CHRISTIAN PROVINCE OF ONTARIO WE CONSIDER THE CENSORSHIP OF GOSPEL MESSAGES WHICH CONTAIN NEITHER ACRIMONY SLANDER OR ABUSE BUT POSITIVE NEW TESTAMENT TEACHING A MOST FLAGRANT DESPOTIC UNJUST AND UNCHRISTIAN RULING TO WHICH A LIBERTY-LOVING BRITISH CANADIAN PUBLIC WILL NOT EASILY SUBMIT IT IS SUCH HIGH HANDED ACTION ON THE PART OF PAID SERVANTS OF THE STATE THAT ENDANGER BRITISH DEMOCRACY AND ENCOURAGE FANATICAL EXTREMISTS WE THEREFORE RESPECTFULLY CALL UPON YOU RIGHT HONOURABLE SIR AS THE ELECTED HEAD OF THIS FREE BRITISH COMMONWEALTH THE DOMINION OF CANADA TO CURB THE INFLUENCES THAT ARE BEHIND SUCH OPPRESSIVE MEASURES DIRECTED AGAINST THE PROTESTANT MAJORITY OF THIS PROVINCE OF ONTARIO.
REV M ZEIDMAN
PRESBYTERIAN MINISTER, ORGANIZER AND DIRECTOR OF THE PROTESTANT RADIO LEAGUE
307 PALMERSTON BLVD TORONTO

If this furor wasn't bad enough, the CBC then discovered they had also backed themselves into another religious dispute. Father Lanphier, a Roman Catholic priest broadcasting from the Radio League of St. Michael's, had a habit of ad-libbing between portions of his script. When the CBC asked the priest to refrain from these off-the-cuff comments, the enraged Knights of Columbus made the Orangemen's protests to the CBC look pale by comparison. A look at the CBC files shows that as there was no reasonable position taken by any of the people involved in either of these episodes, it was almost

Milton Cross broadcast the Texaco-sponsored opera from his box at the Metropolitan for 43 years.

impossible to arrive at solutions. Finally, in order to placate the clergy the CBC turned over the sharing of responsibility for church broadcasts to a national religious advisory council which serves this function to this very day.

In 1936 music filled 70 percent of the CBC schedule, or about seven hours of programming a day, on all of the CBC stations. By 1941 the CBC was broadcasting eighteen hours of music across the country representing about 51 percent of the schedule. Classical music and opera were still a large part of the programming compared to the present day. The Metropolitan Opera broadcasts started Christmas Day 1931 with Deems Taylor talking *over* the music to describe the action, an impossible method which was used only once. Milton Cross followed him as announcer and continued without a break for 850 broadcasts, missing two broadcasts when his wife died. He returned

Ettore Mazzoleni

Healey Willan

Edward Johnson (met director)

Composer Healey Willan examines the score of his opera "Deirdre of the Sorrows", commissioned by the CBC in 1943.

The lead soloists gather for rehearsal of "Deirdre", the first full-length Canadian opera ever written.

Classical music was always a large part of radio programming and the Hart House Quartet were heard often.

and never missed a broadcast again until his own death January 3, 1975 at 77 years of age. It's perhaps not generally known that Milton Cross's delightful ad libs were written by Geri Souvainne, a lady who claims to be "at the top of the Metropolitan Opera's bitch list." That's quite a statement from a lady who's competing with some of the world's most temperamental opera stars. Texaco, which began sponsoring the program in 1940 is the longest continuing sponsor on radio—the saviours of the Met and of the sanity of opera-lovers in North America. The broadcast is still on 48 stations in Canada and 240 in the u.s. It still starts at 2 P.M. and all stations have to promise to carry the whole opera without interference and the whole season without failure. Even though the CBC is no longer in the commercial radio business, the remaining commercial programs are the operas. How sensible of the CBC — how sensible of Texaco.

The "Proms" were a series of musical programs broadcast by the CBC from Varsity Arena in Toronto conducted by Reginald Stewart. Similar concerts were broadcast in Montreal from Mount Royal. Youngsters were often bundled in the family Ford and driven to the road under the chalet to hear the music on a hot summer's night. Toronto Mendelssohn Choir under the direction of Dr. Fricker performed the whole B Minor Mass by Bach in 1939

Alan Young, (above left) a popular Canadian radio comedian, had his first show at the age of fifteen.

and both NBC and CBC carried this concert. On October 23, 1938, "A Musical Portrait of Canada" was broadcast to a world audience, and singers and orchestras were represented from across Canada. Christmas of 1939 was also the first of the famous "Messiah" broadcasts.

Toronto's singers received encouragement because of the Mendelssohn Choir and operas, and soloists were performing on some good radio recitals. Frances James sang a recital at Banff before the Queen and during the Royal Tour Bill Morton, Jack Reid, John Harcourt and Ernest Berry founded the quartet "The Four Gentlemen" which was popular for years.

The Hart House String quartet led the parade of chamber players, which included the McGill Quartet, LeQuatour Jean L'Allemand, L'Ensemble Instrumental de Montreal, The Tudor Quartet of Winnipeg and the Jean de Rimanoczy's string ensemble of Vancouver. Five days a week there were also recitals with classical artists. Organ recitals included a collection of greats

 Radio round tables and forums became a feature of Canadian broadcasting during the '40s. M. J. Coldwell is shown at mike.

such as Ernest MacMillan, Healey Willan, Quentin MacLean, Syd Kelland of Vancouver, Henry Gagnon of Quebec and Hugh Bancroft of Winnipeg.

In a lighter vein, the CBC aired a group of excellent orchestras and leaders with Percy Faith, Alan MacIver, Giuseppi Agostini, Geoff Waddington, Percy Harvey, Albert Pratz and Samuel Hersenhoren. "Let's go to the Music Hall" a Canadian version of an English music hall, was popular and dance bands were heard on a regular basis on the network. Len Hopkins was in Ottawa, Mart Kenny in Vancouver, Don Turner in Montreal, and Toronto had two big bands, Horace Lapp and Luigi Romanelli.

One of the most successful Vancouver programs of the period was "Stag Party" which included Alan Young, who was only fifteen years old when he was first featured. "Stag Party" became the "Alan Young Show" in 1940 and was sponsored by Buckingham cigarettes with announcer Herb May who, if memory serves, did Buckingham commercials years later. Also in the cast were Bernie Braden, a seventeen-year-old Juliette, and Louise Grant.

Mary Grannan,
the popular Canadian writer
and performer of "Just Mary".

The show was broadcast on the network and when the production was moved to Toronto, Juliette stayed in the west and the songs were performed by Charlie Jordan. By 1944 Alan Young had been lured to the u.s. for his own American program on ABC sponsored by Bristol Myers.

Talk broadcasts were always popular on the CNR, CRBC and the CBC because it was a cheap source of programming as well as a soapbox for frustrated reformers and would-be writers. It would seem that the BBC was responsible for "the expert complex" which required each speaker to be an authority on his subject. The list of early radio speakers in Canada is a Who's Who of experts like Davidson Dunton, editor of the *Montreal Standard*, B.K. Sandwell, editor of *Saturday Night*, H.L. Stewart of Dalhousie University and many more. Years later when Don Sims produced a man-on-the-street program called "What's Your Beef" everybody sat up and took notice because non-experts were finally being allowed on the air.

Round tables and Forums were also popular in this period. "Citizen's Forum" which lasted more than twenty-six years started in the fall of 1939, and was produced in co-operation with the Canadian Association for Adult Education. It organized local listeners to hear the broadcast and then discuss the issues after hearing the experts on the network. The Couchiching Conferences were an outgrowth of this type of program.

93

Women like Claire Wallace took an ever-increasing part in radio commentating at this time.

Probably the best-remembered children's program of the Silver Era was the "Just Mary" show featuring Mary Grannan, a school teacher from Fredericton who became interested in radio. After a year of local programming "Just Mary" was moved to the CBC network, and by 1940 Mary Grannan had moved to Toronto where she wrote several other programs including "Maggie Muggins". Lou Snider played the organ for years on her programs, and it was a unique team based on compatibility. Mary was also a close friend of Frank Willis who cheered her up when she was feeling depressed. She was famous for her large hats and enormous earrings, and she was one of the best-liked members of the Toronto radio colony. She retired in April of 1960 and died fifteen years later at the age of seventy-five.

School broadcasts began in British Columbia and Nova Scotia early after the CBC was formed and were gradually produced across the country for various school systems. Eventually a national school broadcast was set up by the CBC, and it's function was to produce expensive Shakespearian dramas and major music programs, shows too costly for regional production. It is one of the few systems existing in Canada where educators can communicate across provincial borders.

Meanwhile in the political and commercial arena the pressure was building on the CBC to give up its sustaining broadcast time for more commercial and popular programs. Within the CBC there was also frustration in the program units because there was not enough air time to develop new programs. So the CBC did the simplest and most practical thing—it started a second radio network.

The CBC network was to be supplemented by a second network with all but the "mother" station in Toronto to be privately owned. The old CBC network became "The Trans Canada Network" and the new network was called "The Dominion Network". The CBC took over the broadcast frequency of CFRB who screamed bloody murder even though they had held the frequency pending CBC's use. They conveniently "forgot" this condition and continued that great national sport, "blaming the CBC" but the CBC persevered and CFRB prospered on their newly assigned frequency.

The war had ended, there were now two Canadian radio networks and a lot of frustrations had been removed for radio staff and advertisers. Time on the air was available to "counter schedule" so that one network could program classical music and the other could have variety programming or drama. As radio's Silver Era came to an end and the Golden Age of Canadian radio began, the talent drain stopped. There was too much work at home and not enough skilled actors and performers to do it. It looked as if radio in Canada had finally come of age. If the Silver Era had trained the performers, it would be the Golden Age that employed them. From 1944 to 1954 there would be superb radio programs with excellent performers. It was television which would bring an end to the happiest and most creative time of radio people's lives.

Early radio studios, curtained and draped to improve sound, resembled the interior of a casket.

Radio and the Stars...
Trade Secrets Revealed!

When radio first began, listeners were grateful to hear any sound at all coming from their sets. But when the technology of radio had improved beyond the squeak and squabble stage, when microphones had been improved so that the sounds of musical instruments were readily distinguishable, it became obvious that the content of programs had finally become important.

The first radio plays were produced by active theatre groups from material already prepared for the stage, and the music performed for these shows was the same as the musicians played at the hotels or dance halls which employed them. After a time it became apparent that special material was needed for radio—that it was a new and different medium needing new treatment. Radio productions began when the search started for original radio material.

Until then, the director was often an actor in the play performed and the "engineer" controlled the microphone as he thought best, not always with the director's intentions in mind. In musical programs the situation was even worse. Because some engineers did not understand music, emphasis for a particular instrument or section of the orchestra would be misplaced; for example, sometimes during a violin solo the trumpets would take over. There was an obvious need for supervision, and as a result, at least one musician in Canada became a radio director. John Adaskin began his career as a cellist under the direction of Geoff Waddington. When the engineer asked Geoff for advice John would go into the control room and listen. The programs improved so much with his help that he was often booked for a broadcast, but told to leave his cello at home. He thus evolved into a producer/director.

A radio production studio in the 1920s. The microphone is hidden in the lamp so that performers wouldn't be intimidated by it.

When dramas started on radio in Canada they were primarily the work of amateurs. In Vancouver they were performed mainly by English theatre people who had immigrated to Western Canada. When the CNR brought Tyrone Guthrie from the U.K. to produce the Romance of Canada series in Montreal, he discovered that he had to teach some of the theatre actors how to work with microphones. Since he was expected to deliver some programs almost immediately, he instituted a double system. According to Austin Weir, the program director for CNR at that time, for each hour of rehearsal Guthrie required an hour of radio school for his actors. To complicate matters, almost all of his actors had full time jobs during the day, so they could only work nights or weekends. Therefore, most rehearsals were from 7 P.M. to 11 P.M. It took four nights of rehearsal and four nights of school for each production.

At that time programs were produced in two studios. Actors were in A and sound effects were in B with the control room between them. The original radio studios were built like the interior of a casket, which they resembled. Drapes and curtains were moved around mysteriously by experts to improve the sound. Later new microphones did a better job than new drapes and the studio evolved into a rather austere sound-proofed room where the actors performed.

In this early radio photo, two microphones are hidden in the globe.

When Canadian drama productions began on CNR they were controlled by Englishmen in Vancouver and Montreal, and therefore BBC production methods were used. When CNR dropped its radio network because of the Depression, there was a hiatus in radio dramas and when drama was resumed it was under the aegis of the CRBC, and producers, writers and directors began to adopt American production methods.

Basically, the difference between the British and American productions was established by the dominance of the radio engineer. In the BBC they run the show—in America the producer runs the show! In the U.K. the actors were in one studio, the orchestra in another and the sound-effects men in the third. The actors had to take visual cues from the director and required very specific and exact directions in order to integrate their voices with the music and sound. This was ideal for the engineers who had to control the volumes of the various parts but it required monumental imagination on the part of the actors. Since so much skill was required the BBC employed a repertory company of actors, and the producers were required to draw on this stock company for their basic casts although they could book their lead actors from the freelance colony.

Radio needed cheap ways to produce shows and sing-songs filled the bill.

In America radio never got hung up on the technical problems. The early radio plays were done in theatres with audiences and therefore all the elements of a broadcast were on stage and visible. What took hours to rehearse without music and sound now took minutes as the actors listened to the sounds and co-ordinated their acting to the sounds. Sound men could see the actors and "feel" the action. Lux Radio Theatre and the Ford Radio theatre are examples of staged radio plays of this time. Everybody on stage was well dressed to set the theatre mood. Upstage was a large orchestra of from twenty to forty musicians in black tie and tails. On the sides were the chorus of singers (if needed) and at the front of the stage the key microphone.

There were three levels of programs in the u.s. The first level was the star vehicle such as "Lux Radio Theatre" with Cecil B. deMille introducing favourite actors performing radio versions of their current movies. The stars were often terrible radio actors needing long rehearsals. Five days before the broadcast the actors read through the play, discussed character and adjusted the script. The following days, rehearsals were slow as the stars learned microphone techniques. The day before the performance the orchestra was added for a day-long rehearsal and perhaps a rough dress rehearsal. On the day of the program there was a dress rehearsal which was recorded and studied before the program went on the air "live".

The next level of drama programming was the studio adventure which was complete in just one or two days depending on the format and the talents

100

An early two-man "walkie-talkie" radio team covering a golf tournament.

of the actors. "Gang Busters" took two days because there was no music at the scene change and all of the bridges were complex sound effects. A simple adventure or mystery like "Inner Sanctum" was done in one day, including read-through, rehearsal and broadcast. These programs were generally excellently produced and used top actors who were relatively well paid for their efforts. Many of these actors went on to Hollywood stardom, including Van Heflin, William Powell and Orson Welles.

Lowest on the drama scale came the "soaps". These productions were produced in the studio in a short period of time, and they all had one purpose, to make money. Soap-opera actors had to be tremendously disciplined just to survive because most "soaps" were produced in two hours from start to finish, but since many had fixed casts there was little or no work done on character interpretation. These productions also had one major disadvantage if they were produced in New York; they had to be done twice, first at the scheduled eastern time and then two or three hours later "for the west". Many an actor on his way home risked his life rushing back to the New York studios as he had "forgotten to feed to the west".

One of the earliest series of radio drama produced in Canada which had lagged far behind the u.s. for a number of reasons already mentioned earlier

101

CBC's Reid Forsee (behind desk) teaches radio voice techniques to ministers and priests in 1946.

in the book, was a series of Shakespeare's plays produced in Vancouver in 1929 by the CNRV players. They also put on one evening of original Canadian plays but no record exists of the authors of the plays.

In the early 1930s Andrew Allan was hired by Toronto's CFRB as an announcer but Allan's main interest had always revolved around drama and he began producing and writing radio plays for the station. Although he was given a small budget for writers there was no money to pay actors for the shows so the group who hung out at Murray's Restaurant near the Toronto studio worked solely for the experience. In those days actors were so anxious to get radio experience that it was possible for Edgar Stone to set up a non-broadcasting Radio Hall where he produced plays. Bob Christie and Rai Purdy were two of his successful students, and eventually, Toronto stations transmitted some of these productions.

Lucio Agostini

A typical radio stage layout of the late '40s shows the music area separated from the actors.

The CBC made Rupert Lucas head of drama in 1938, and by 1939 Lucas decided professional acting colonies were needed in Montreal, Toronto, Winnipeg and Vancouver, to provide actors for the radio dramas he would create. But the basis of Lucas's acting colonies grew out of the Farm Broadcasts produced daily at noon.

By the 1950s most half-hour network dramas were employing fully professional performers and required only three and a half hours of rehearsal to produce and broadcast. An hour-long program took seven to nine hours rehearsal. In 1953 the "Stage Series" rehearsals took $5^{1}/_{2}$ hours on Saturday with another $3^{1}/_{2}$ on Sunday for the "live" broadcast at 9 P.M. that night. The few quarter-hour soaps including "Brave Voyage" took less than 3 hours to rehearse and broadcast and the farm soap opera "The Craigs" only took a half-hour. The cast ran through the script just once and then taped the program.

103

Dramas before tape were like a theatre experience, with all the elements coming together at one place at one time. As can be imagined, they were hard on the nerves but great fun as well. In present-day productions the producer frequently employs actors to "track" parts of the program and the producer then takes the voice tracks and adds music, other voices and sound effects later in the editing session. This requires a more skilled producer who can draw on an actor's talents in a different manner. It also gives the producer absolute control but deprives the actor of a great deal of creative involvement and pleasure.

The relationship between the CBC producers and performers always had three basic unwritten principles—trust, subterfuge and tact. Until the advent of television there seldom was a written contract for an actor or writer in the CBC. This level of trust shocked auditors and lawyers when they saw the amount of money paid actors with only verbal agreement—no bills, no invoices and no contracts. It worked.

Because it was the producer's responsibility to find out what an actor usually got paid without insulting the actor by asking, subterfuge was always necessary. Certain actors were paid for all of their parts at overscale while others were paid union scale, although there was no discrimination in pay for a lead or bit player. On the other side of the coin, actors were expected to know which show could pay over scale and which shows paid scale. A show with regular work at scale would often be considered far more valuable than an occasional lead part at overscale. For example, Frank Peddie accepted scale for playing "old man Craig" in the daily farm broadcast, because he considered this part "bread and butter".

Tact was an essential part of a producer's personality. While our CBC colony was a puritan group compared to modern swingers, there were always some alliances in the making or breaking stages. The producer was expected to have knowledge of these relationships so that he would not cast ex-lovers together in a passionate radio love scene. But the producers did not pry into an actor's life. There were reliable sources at the CBC—a few minutes with the secretaries regularly gave a producer more information than he could ever use. The actors were equally friendly to these sources of wisdom and an effective system of communication was maintained for years.

Customs and traditions also developed based on the quirks of the performers, producers and musicians. Just as theatre is loaded with traditions so did radio develop its own. When the CBC used the concert studio on McGill Street, for years Tommy Tweed always sat in the same chair away from the other actors, and no one would consider sitting in that seat if Tommy was around. When he retired his friends gave him the theatre seat as a happy souvenir of his career.

Actors were required to be at rehearsal fifteen minutes before the call in

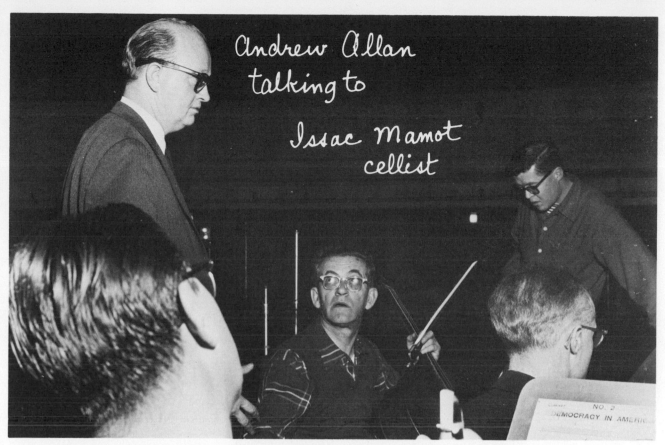

*Andrew Allan
talking to

Issac Mamot
cellist*

Radio musicians took a personal interest in "their" shows.

order to be ready to give their full attention to the rehearsal. As a courtesy, most producers would conveniently arrive five minutes after "call" so that the late-comers could sneak in. Some actors like Jane Mallett were always late, and it became a custom to wait for her delightful, funny but believable reason for tardiness.

The radio acting colony also stuck together and helped each other out. The actor Herb Gott was in an accident when he was a young man and lost both his arms, and this was kept secret for many years. There are several publicity pictures of Herb cleverly set up so nobody would be aware of this, and the whole colony of actors combined to help Herb in all of the small ways they could.

While the actors welcomed new, talented performers like Barry Morse they were cruel to those without ability or manners. An actor of some talent once got booked by Frank Willis for a secondary lead. The young man arrived late, lost his script, jumped actors' cues, placed his script so that other actors couldn't get near the mike and was generally inconsiderate. One of the cast protested privately to Frank, but when he did not take the complaints seriously, other performers started their own private war on the offender. The actors deliberately mixed his voice inflections with theirs so that the listeners could

105

 From the actors' point of view: Esse Ljungh in production booth.

 *From Ljungh's point of view: actors Beth Lockerbie and Frank Peddie.*

Baffle to cut sound from orchestra

Albert Pratz (conductor)

girl chorus

Rod Coneybeare (announcer)

Jack Kane (arranger)

A "work through" rehearsal for "Let's Make Music" checking for notes, timing and interpretation.

not hear one of his speeches end and another begin. Frank finally had to reduce his part to almost nothing, and that actor seldom worked for the CBC again. I'm sure he never knew what the others were doing to him.

Every producer/director had his own special methods with the actors and Andrew Allan often resorted to the "whipping boy" technique — an unpleasant surprise for new actors. A "whipping boy" is an actor who is "picked on" or over-directed so that the producer gives direction to other actors through him. When Andrew came out of the control room and walked to the actor's microphone, everyone knew a "whipping" was in store. Although a frightening experience it had its compensation in regular employment, however.

While drama productions presented certain problems, musical and variety programs had different needs and required different production techniques. Most producers were better fans than musicians and their job came second to that of the orchestra leader. In a music program there was only one boss — the conductor, and the producer's job was mainly to create an atmosphere for the conductor and musicians. A message from the producer to singers came through the conductor, and as most conductors wore earphones the producer could talk to the conductor without the rest of the studio group hearing the directions.

An Esse Ljungh radio production.

Sometimes producers had control over timing and pacing of a musical program but even this was generally delegated privately to the conductor. To the bystander the producer often appeared a flunky of the conductor, but this was not the case. Producers wielded enormous power over music programs but always in the privacy of their offices, and any battles between producers and conductors were fought there. But conductors knew that if a producer hired him it was because he considered the conductor talented—this was the basis of the fan-master relationship and it usually worked. Most producers also left the rehearsal controls to the musical leader who generally coached the singers unless there was a vocal coach. The producer's role was as a timer or adjudicator, and he seldom directed performers in their technical performances and never directed them in interpretation—this was left up to the conductor.

Variety shows were a different matter again and control was split among the dominant personalities in a program. Pop music programs were custom-made to suit the stars. Jazz for example, with Moe Koffman starring, featured Moe's ideas and taste. But a complex production of lush big sounds, choruses and soloists was frequently the producer's total responsibility because he had to unite so many personalities. "Let's Make Music" split the duties between the producer John Kannawin, the conductor Albert Pratz and the writer-narrator, Rod Coneybeare. Talent shows in the 1940s like "Opportunity Knocks" were run by the conductor, John Adaskin. Bert Pearl was the boss on the Happy Gang and nobody forgot it. On the Wayne and Shuster show

108

Ford Radio Theatre cast on stage. Behind scenes in control booth producer Alan Savage and operator Mary Muir.

the "boys" were clearly in charge as they are on their television programs. Jackie Rae, their radio producer, had a lot to say about the production, but John and Frank decided what was funny. Certain small studio productions were the responsibility of the main voice, and Bert Devitt and Uncle Bod are examples. All of the production efforts had to meet the exact tastes of the star. Bod worked directly with Lou Snider on the organ and with the sound-effects man. Mary Sime played the piano and took instructions from Bert Devitt on Bert's late-night show "Escape With Me". Mary, of course, was Bert's buddy "Smitty", the man Bert talked to throughout the show.

Certain booth productions were produced by the announcers, and production was and still is, part of a network announcer's job. Certain talk shows were dominated by the producer while others were controlled by the star. Kate Aitken rigidly controlled her broadcasts though the sponsor hired the organist, Horace Lapp, and the announcer Cy Strange. Kate would breeze into the studio close to broadcast time, pass around her script, rehearse five minutes (for a fifteen-minute program), then go on the air. She always finished on time and smiling.

Political talks in Toronto were generally produced by Reid Forsee who was a master of diplomacy. Many politicians had a low regard for the CBC and it was Reid's job to make them conform to CBC regulations. This was not

BROADCASTER MAGAZINE

Toronto women commentators of the '50s. (Left to right) Kate Aitken, June Dennis, Jane Weston, Wendy Paige, Mona Gould.

always easy. Many Conservative candidates or MPs were convinced that the CBC was a hive of communists but once they encountered Forsee's charm they were always satisfied they had at least one friend in the CBC. Liberals were so confident under Mackenzie King that they walked around the CBC as if it was their private preserve, but Reid tactfully made them aware of CBC's independence.

CBC talk shows were controlled by a Talks and Public Affairs group, and the problems of political balance were endlessly discussed and rigidly checked out. An extraordinary collection of intellectuals loyally bound together by an admiration for good talk-show productions, each producer of the talk group cultivated contacts all over Canada and the world. Combined they had unlimited access to good speakers.

The CBC tolerated advertising agency producers but did not encourage them. If advertising agencies were responsible to the sponsors for programs the shows also had to meet CBC standards. Some agencies had excellent producers working for them while some sponsors and agencies preferred to use CBC producers including Esse Ljungh, Jackie Rae and Andrew Allan. These producers were paid extra fees for agency productions, and Esse Ljungh used to earn an extra $30,000 a year in the early 1950s for General Electric Showtime, Brave Voyage and the Ronson Show. Agencies were always convinced that the CBC technicians needed financial support too and often slipped extra fees to the crews. This was always welcome especially when the crew's salaries averaged out at only $2,500 per annum during the 1950s.

For a great many years CBC radio producers all over Canada were expected to produce all kinds of programs. Only the super-producers like Caplan, Allan, Gibbs and Ray Whitehouse specialized in drama or music. The rest including Esse Ljungh, were required to produce whatever they were assigned. Until about 1955, the Toronto group consisted of seventeen producers, who produced two full network schedules. It was not a job for the meek or the slow — producers often worked full-out seven days a week and always on public holidays — nevertheless, a producer's job was so coveted that we never complained — besides we were having too much fun.

Radio reporters often showed up in unlikely places. Here's one waiting for a political bigwig to pass by (or over).

In the placid fifties, all-girl choirs like the Leslie Bell singers were radio favorites.

RADIO'S GOLDEN AGE 1944-1954

Hello Out There
in Radioland!

Canada's Golden Age in radio began in January 1944 and lasted for ten delightful years. Radio personalities who are still part of the present-day scene and programs which became national institutions came out of those magnificent years. The Happy Gang had a devoted audience across Canada, those zany comics Wayne and Shuster made all Canada laugh and CBC's Wednesday nights became must-listening for the country's intellectuals. It was also during this period that Canadian listeners heard Andrew Allen's "Stage" series and first became aware that radio theatre could actually be a special, vital part of the creative world.

Today's sentimentalists may rhapsodize over unsponsored programs like "Jake and the Kid" which had a very small audience when it was originally produced but they've forgotten the popular commercial successes of the time like G.E. Showtime, and Ford Radio Theatre. And it was commercial radio which gave impetus to the talents of Lucio Agostini, Andrew Allen, Esse Ljungh, and John Drainie. Canadian writers of the time also had the chance to introduce audiences to the country's heritage and customs . . . men like Bill Mitchell with his prairie stories, and Charles Wasserman with the kooky patois of Ti Jean.

There were, however, two things that did not come from the Golden Age —stars and scripts that will endure forever. When reviewing scripts from this time, drama critics have commented that not many of them "hold up" when they are re-read. But the critics have missed the point—they forget that these scripts were not intended to "hold up." They were written *of* and *for* their time. The radio plays by Len Peterson, Bill Mitchell, Bill Strange and George Salverson were successful just because they were relevant to the times and the listeners.

Amateur hours on radio always featured the inevitable tap dancer.

As for "stars" they were a luxury Canadian radio couldn't afford. A "star" is someone who stays at home and waits for exactly the right part while the "flunkies" slave over hot microphones. Our "stars" were far too busy playing too many parts to ever fit the category.

Although there were now two networks in Canada, listeners were not aware that much had changed. Granted that they could now hear the top American programs on the Trans Canada or Dominion network rather than turning to an American station, they still turned to their local stations for most of their entertainment. There were significant differences between the two networks with the Dominion carrying most of the big expensive commercial shows and the Trans Canada concentrating more on the "sustaining" highbrow programs. But as the local stations used network shows for "prime time" (evening) programming listeners remained unaware of which network was involved. Local stations used local talent for other than "prime time" or from sign on at 6 A.M., before lunch and dinner time. And regardless of whether the station had Dominion or Trans Canada affiliates, all radio stations had certain common elements during this period.

A child performer on local amateur radio show. The judge was usually the local movie house manager.

A study of the schedules discloses these facts: All stations had Bulova Watch time checks. All stations did "remotes" from the local dance hall on Saturday night followed by a religious program broadcast from the local church on Sunday morning. All stations had a "story lady" or "uncle" who gave out free pop and cake to the kids in the studio. All stations had a local talent show with the inevitable tap dancers judged by the local movie manager because he was in "showbiz". Most stations had a local "professional musician who played the piano or organ as well as a "distinguished" news commentator and, of course, "sports celebrity". There was always a women's commentator "helped" by a male announcer and all stations really tried and usually succeeded in understanding their listeners and giving them both the entertainment they wanted and the information they needed.

If all radio programming of the time was predictable, the staff, or more correctly, the cast of characters at each station was just as predictable. The morning wake-up man on the air from 6 to 9 A.M. was the highest-paid station employee and usually the biggest cheapskate. Because he was the local star he was invited everywhere—he might be a poorly educated slob but one thing he always had was *personality*.

Teen dances were big on private radio stations in the '50s and supplied cheap programming. Prizes donated were records supplied free to the stations.

Except for "dry" stations like Chatham, each station had a resident drunk, usually a down-and-out actor who always reminded everyone how he could have been a star in the "big city". The station newsman was either the chief announcer, program director or both and he always had a deep, dark voice. If he did indeed sound as if he was ten feet tall he was more than likely just over five feet, had no chin and wore thick glasses. The chief announcer would always broadcast the dance remotes and "big stuff" and he was the guy who had the best chance to make it with the local belles.

The late-night man was frequently the junior announcer who always believed himself to be sexy and often read soupy poetry to violin music. The local opera or church soloist was always the best announcer at the station. He'd have a magnificent voice and was the only announcer on staff who could pronounce the names of the classical composers correctly.

The news commentator was always highly educated, condescending and either sounded British or was. The women's commentator usually doubled as the "story lady" and was often an unfulfilled actress, frequently an alcoholic and always had a "broken marriage". The sportscaster worked for the local paper and was often an ex-athlete trying desperately to relive the days of glory. The chief operator never stopped working, helling and talking. He wrote memos that begged the other operators "don't say it to me—write it" but it was hopeless because none of his operators ever knew how to write. The chief engineer was, and always will be, a grouch.

Each station had five sources of programs: local live, network, transcribed programs, transcription services and records. There is a difference between a transcribed program and transcription services by the way, which I'll explain.

While the listener could spot a local live program, some "transcribed programs" sounded just like network programs. However the law required the transcribed programs to include the word "transcribed" somewhere in the program. Transcribed programs were complete programs recorded generally in the u.s. in New York or Los Angeles on 16-inch recordings and copied on a 16-inch transcription. Each side of the disc had fifteen minutes of program. These shows included adventure programs like "Superman", "Orphan Annie", and the "Green Hornet". Some of these programs were controlled by sponsors including "This Is My Story" by the Salvation Army or "Orphan Annie" by Ogilvie Cereals. Once a station had broadcasted the program which they leased for $10 to $100 for each 15-minute side they shipped them to the next station to be used again.

"Transcription services" were 16-inch discs of colourful plastic, which supplied the ingredients to make a program—music, scripts, production bridges, weather reports, etc. Each transcription had several cuts or items on each side much like the modern long-playing record. The total time for each piece was printed on the label along with the "copyright" information for clearance as well as the usual information about the title and artists. Some labels showed the number of seconds of music before the singer or voice started so that the announcer could "talk over" right up to the vocal.

Some of these transcription programs, especially the Sunday afternoon programs, were complex productions with mood bridges and modulations and most of these programs had a theme: "rivers," or "spring," or "lovers"— a kind of forerunner of Mantovani.

For holidays and special occasions like Halloween and Christmas there were beautifully researched scripts about "Santa Claus around the World" or "How Cupid Got Involved on St. Valentine's Day." Some transcription services supplied orchestral backgrounds with a choice of three different keys and songs for disc jockeys to sing in the morning or late night. Many a disc jockey serenaded his audience with "White Christmas" or "Don't Fence Me In" accompanied by the best orchestras in the world.

A small station with a miniscule budget could sound like a big network station if they had a good transcription service. If the law hadn't required the word "transcribed" or "recorded" the listener would have been convinced the program was from an enormous auditorium with a huge audience because the services also included recorded applause.

Above photo shows complex mobile coverage at Jamboree '55, the International Scout Rally. This was a good layout for multiple language broadcasting. The CBC supplied technical know-how and equipment and the visiting broadcasters did their own commentary. Events were recorded as they happened and the tracks were mixed with each language.

The transcription services were American, distributed in Canada by special agents. The service included storage cabinets, scripts, production advice, weather and time jingles; supplementary transcriptions of new material and scripts were also supplied each month. The best known services were Standard, Langworth, Thesaurus (NBC's service) and World. These services were contracted for a minimum of two years and cost the station between $100 and $500 a month depending on the size of the market or station location.

The straight script services for local drama productions were available to most stations from American distributors and were usually excellent. They

118

Jane Mallett

Beth Lockerbie

Syd Brown

Peggy Brown

Jack Scott

Cast of Canadian soap opera "Brave Voyage" posed in Esse Ljungh's living room.

were re-writes of good American radio plays re-written by the original author. A syndicated service sold the scripts and the performing rights for as little as $7 and as high as $1,000.

Another program service to radio stations was news service from the Canadian Press, a co-operative owned by many Canadian newspapers that distributed news across the country by teletype on a regular basis. When radio became an important customer they created the B.N.S. (the Broadcast News Service) which supplied complete newscasts typed on the receiving teletype and supposedly ready for reading. Along with the news service came "hints for cooking", "famous birthdays" and terrible jokes . . . "What is a pig skin most used for?"—"To hold the pig together." Now you know where disc jockeys get their material. But since the C.P. newscasts supplied mostly regional information, stations usually had a news room, and if the radio

119

Radio station announcers were expected to drive the boldly-marked station cars carefully.

station was owned by a newspaper the news staff generally came from the paper.

Announcers during the Golden Age were a highly-trained group with special talents. A staff of announcers was divided into groups from disc jockeys to "serious" announcers who did the news and classical music commentary. They were all supported by script services and therefore hardly ever "talked"—they "announced". A comparison to contemporary announcing is not fair because now all announcers, with few exceptions, are "personalities" which requires less training and very little script service support. When announcers did not have script services or writers they were required to write their own scripts on such programs as dance remotes. Ad libs were frowned upon. Even when announcers pulled their own records for a record program they "balanced" the show and then wrote a script.

Announcers of that time, were also expected to develop an expertise in sports, agriculture, music or theatre. They were also required to drive the boldly marked station car with care and courtesy and wear the station blazer "emblazoned" with the station crest. Station management was fussy about

Gordon Sinclair, Kate Aitken, Bob Weston and Cy Strange, a powerhouse group of radio talent in the fifties.

their men and required utmost courtesy from them at all times. It goes without saying that when the announcer did the "church remote" he was expected not to smoke in the organ loft. The skill required to conceal his bad habits caused some real strain for an announcer but it wasn't all slavery. There were some real benefits. Nice ladies sent cookies and mitts to him and not-so-nice ladies made different offers. The local movies let him in free with his date to "review" the latest show, and dance hall operators often set up drinks for the "crew" during the Saturday-night broadcast. He got the best table at the local bootlegger's, and record companies gave him free records in order to get them played. Local sponsors were under the misapprehension that an announcer had lots of money and would offer him deals for cars, furniture and other unattainable luxuries, but station management was aware of all these "perks" and included their value in salaries. As a result their salaries were so low that a junior announcer simply could not afford to get married and in some cases had to move from one station to another to get a raise of as little as $3 a week.

In fact, the entire staff of a radio station was so engrossed with their "status" that the idea of working long hours with little money was acceptable. They were always "on" and if they saw a fire or other newsworthy event they'd find the nearest booth and phone the newsroom. In the event of a disaster or "big story" they were all expected to automatically turn up at the station to help. Staff ate, breathed and lived radio twenty-four hours a day, seven days a week, worked week-ends for the big productions and on all holidays such as Christmas, New Years and Thanksgiving. Because they worked so hard broadcast parties were used as occasions for a lot of hard drinking and high-stake gambling. At my first experience with one of these sessions I nearly choked on my beer when one of the station brass cheerfully lost his car in a game of craps.

The conversation at these parties always revolved around work and it was not unusual for some of the group to leave and go to the station in the middle of the night to experiment on an idea suggested at the party. In fact all-night experimenting was common for announcers and technicians who worked on new sounds and ideas and then signed on the station at six the next morning. Sometimes the staff would leave a party and go to the station to sleep until the wakeup crew arrived and it was an understood rule in all radio stations that no one was ever to turn on a microphone in a darkened studio. Who knew what shenanigans were going on with some sweet young thing on the piano cover?

Radio staff have always had vivid imaginations and there have grown up a series of legends about studio hi-jinx, some of them true, some false. For example, the legend that women commentators were stripped in the studio while reading their 15-minute items is false. Most women announcers sat down to read their broadcasts. Have you ever tried stripping a woman sitting down? Can't be done, guys. Switching on radio performers early to catch swearing "on the air" was reputedly very funny. My one experience with this ruse shocked me and the whole studio — there was so much competition for radio jobs that anyone swearing on the air was fired. Even a deviation from a script was considered a serious error — who could laugh at the prospect of someone losing his job?

There was some basis for the legends about stripping men announcers while they were broadcasting. This generally consisted of opening his fly and undoing his belt, while the announcer stood at the mike to get those deep, sonorous sounds he treasured. On occasion an announcer did have his script set on fire while he was reading, and stories about operators trying to make announcers laugh on the air are true. In most stations the operators and announcers have a "talkback" system so they can communicate without going on the air, and this was used by the operators to try to make an announcer laugh during certain broadcasts. Rude and obscene remarks were

The "Gang" celebrating an anniversary of their popular show. (Left to right) Bert Pearl, Bob Farnon, Hugh Bartlett, Blain Mathe, George Temple, Kay Stokes.

frequently made by the operator to the announcer during commercials and certain types of announcements. The announcers would train themselves to ignore these remarks and seldom had trouble with them. But they could never become completely immune to visual kidding. The operator would go to great lengths to break up the announcer, sometimes even stripping so he could wave a certain part of his anatomy at the announcer. I always knew how to break up John Rae, a particularly unflappable announcer, who excelled at commercials which included such common phrases as "yes ladies, hurry down to your corner grocery store and save!" I'd hold up a sign which said "Jesus saves — too." It worked everytime.

For legal reasons everything on radio was scripted during the Golden Age and hence it was often possible for operators to lay traps for announcers. When tape recording was perfected the need for scripting ended and a whole style of radio and radio hi-jinxs ended.

SOUND	KNOCK, KNOCK.
BERT	Who's there?
FULL CAST	It's the Happy Gang.
BERT	Well come on in. MUSIC

And all Canada did come in. The Happy Gang was one of the best things to hit Canadian radio. Although their program began in the Silver Age in 1937

123

The Happy Gang cheered Canadian audiences throughout the Depression and the war. (Left to right) Blain Mathe, Bert Pearl, Bob Farnon, George Temple (producer), Kay Stokes.

it wasn't until they transfered from intimate studio productions to the livelier audience participation format produced from the McGill Street studios in Toronto that the show really took off. During the Depression the Canadians appreciated their cheerful music and comedy and during the war they desperately needed it.

Bert Pearl, the founder and driving force of "The Gang", has been described by many writers as a sensitive, deeply involved performer who really believed in the corny poems to "Mom" and the sentimental hearts-and-flowers music on Valentine's Day. But what the reporters missed was Bert's professionalism. Bert worked continuously at improving his show. He employed the best talent he could find, paid them well, and expected them to earn their money.

In February, 1950 *Maclean's Magazine* published an article by June Callwood called "The Not So Happy Gang" in which she revealed the weaknesses of the merrymakers and pointed out the supposed frustrations of the side men Bobby Gimby and Cliff McKay, because they were orchestra leaders on other shows. What Miss Callwood failed to recognize was that an orchestra

Kay Stokes and other "Gang" members were top professional musicians.

leader had no compunction about being a side man on a good show and Bert used top performers and orchestra leaders because he demanded outstanding people on his own show.

The original cast of The Happy Gang consisted of Bert Pearl, Bob Farnon, Blain Mathe and Kay Stokes. Hugh Bartlett was the first announcer, and George Temple was the producer for years. The show's first sponsor was Colgate Palmolive.

All of the cast were successful in their own right before joining "The Gang". Kathleen Stokes was well known as a theatre organist, and Bob Farnon at the age of twenty had already written a symphony. Blain Mathe was a violinist in the Toronto Symphony Orchestra who could also let his hair down and make his fiddle "swing", and Eddie Allan had won a gold medal at the CNE for his accordion playing and had made his radio debut at the age of fifteen as a boy soprano. (Eddie is now living in London, Ontario, and is rumoured to be working on a book about The Happy Gang.)

The talent that came on the show in later years was just as indicative of Bert Pearl's drive to get performers would could survive the show's difficult ad lib environment.

125

 The "Gang" show really took off after audience participation was introduced.

A daily format was all that ever existed as script material. For special events Bert would write a tribute or a special piece of music. The rest of the time the group rehearsed the music only, as everyone on the show knew how it all went together. Special material was often written by other members of the gang as well. Bert Niosi wrote some jazz numbers, including one called "The Brothers". This was played by Bert and his two brothers John, a drummer and Joe who played bass fiddle. Cliff McKay was on the show before going on to TV fame with Holiday Ranch, and Bob Gimby, the Pied Piper of "Ca–na–da" in 1967, was also an early "Gang" member. Among the top piano and organ players who worked on the show were Jimmy Namaro, Lloyd Edwards and Lou Snider, and Les Foster played the accordion from time to time. Blain Mathe and Kathleen Stokes were the only ones out of eleven musicians who were not band leaders.

The program always started with a knock "Who's there?" (full cast) "It's the Happy Gang" — "Well, come on in!" followed by the song "Keep

126

CBC's **HAPPY GANG**
BROADCAST *Daily* MON thru FRI. 1:15 – 1:45 P.M.
on Trans-Canada Network of CBC Radio

RED ROSE COFFEE
Carnation *Evaporated* Milk
WESTONS

Vintage Happy Gang (left to right) Lloyd Edwards, Jimmy Namaro, Joe Niosi, Eddie Allen, Bobby Gimby, Les Foster, (Blain Mathe and Bert Niosi cannot be seen in photo.)

Happy with the Happy Gang" written by Bert Pearl. The items that made up the show were all suited to the talents of the gang. Blain and Kay played duets. Eddie sang and played his accordion. Bert did a lot of the comedy but excelled in sentimental stuff, and everybody contributed to the joke box. The accent on instrumental music featured on the show was a reflection of the time, as popular recordings did not depend as much on vocalists and the band was considered more important until the 1950s. The Happy Gang was such a successful show that broadcasters naturally tried to imitate it — The Liptonaires and the Jolly Miller Show — were examples, but although they were good shows they never succeeded like the Happy Gang. The "Gang" had developed a unique style that has never been equalled and a large, loyal and loving audience that no other show before or since has ever been able to attract. If Canada ever had radio "stars" it was the "Gang".

127

There's no doubt that Johnny Wayne and Frank Shuster also deserve to be called "stars" in a country which has traditionally resisted the star system. Unlike the Happy Gang which could not transfer their ideas to television, the "Wayne and Shuster Show" not only became the first sponsored Canadian program to make it in the top 10 listeners ratings in radio but matched that feat in television.

The "boys" started as a writing team for CFRB in Toronto in 1941. Their first program "Wife Preservers" consisted of household hints, was sponsored by Javex and was heard three times a week. So successful was the team that CFRB moved them into their nighttime schedule in a new variety show, "Co-eds and Cutups". About the same time Maurice Rosenfeld put them on the CBC network with a sponsored program "Blended Rhythm" selling Buckingham cigarettes. But the boys left to join the entertainment unit of the Army during the war and Alan Young of Vancouver who later went on to fame in the U.S., replaced them.

In 1945 John and Frank returned to Canada to write and produce the "Johnny Home Show" a clever and funny propaganda show about repatriation starring Austin Willis, and one year later the boys started "The Wayne and Shuster Show", again sponsored by Buckingham Cigarettes with Herb May as their announcer.

Johnny and Frank wrote all of their own material and even some of their music including their theme "I'm a Booster for Wayne and Shuster". Another theme which was used in their early shows was a swinging version of the American folk song "Frankie and Johnny". Wayne and Shuster's great talent was tested in the United States when they were the summer replacement for the William Bendix show, "The Life of Riley". Their main strength lay in the fact that they wrote all of their own material which included situation-comedy sketches, songs and comedy dramas. They figured that they knew best what they could do best, and so it proved. For support they created a cast of zany characters including a deaf postman played by Bernie Braden and Heathcliff the male war bride played by Eric Christmas. Christmas also played Madame Humperdink who always greeted the boys with a loud exuberant "how do you doo".

Wayne and Shuster set out to be Canadian and not American entertainers and they have always worked from Canada even when doing American network programs. They took this position long before it was fashionable and it is gratifying to see how popular they are in Canada, the country to which they feel such a fierce sense of loyalty.

It was during the Golden Era, that thinking man's radio was given a real boost and CBC's "Wednesday Night" series became mandatory listening for the intellectual and artistic colonies across Canada. Here's an example of what the series produced on their first season: Morris Surdin composed a

Johnny Wayne and Frank Shuster were always boosters for Canada.

129

Lister Sinclair (left) and Andrew Allan (shown here with actress Alice Hill) wrote and produced fine radio drama in the fifties.

musical, The Gallant Greenhorn, written by Ray Darby for the opening night show which was followed by two operas, three of Shakespeare's dramas, a play by Lister Sinclair, a satire by Eric Nicol, a production of Ibsen's Hedda Gabler, a verse play by T. S. Eliot and a show about Saskatchewan's history by Tommy Tweed.

The series later included superb dramatized talk shows such as Ted Pope's "Death on the Barren Grounds", and an original play, "A Beach of Strangers" which won the world's most highly-prized radio award, The Italia for its writer-producer John Reeves. Because of the series, Andrew Allan, Esse Ljungh and Frank Willis also finally got the chance to produce the plays they especially loved.

Harry Boyle, the creator of the series, has probably influenced more broadcasters than anyone else in North America. Harry, who'd had his own problems especially with alcohol, felt that people who had suffered great personal problems were more "sensitive" than the rest of the world. As a result he gave assignments to some astonishing people and it usually worked.

Harry J. Boyle, one of the most influential men in Canadian radio, is now Vice-chairman of the CRTC.

He gave me a two-and-a-half hour epic to produce on the history of the St. Lawrence River when I was only twenty-three years old. Further, he hired my father to write it simply because he and James Bannerman thought it was time for a father-and-son act on the CBC.

Boyle was at constant war with CBC senior management when he was in charge of the Trans Canada Network and hence there was an annual hunt to "get Harry's hide". It seemed inconceivable to them that Harry could run a complete radio network, write, freelance, and drink. At one time when they were sure Harry wouldn't have his fall schedule completed he not only surprised them with a good schedule but gave them a bonus in the way of

top left   *Lister Sinclair, Andrew Allan and Dr. Walter Goldsmith of the University of Southern California.*

top right   *Actors Alan Pearce, Alan King, Barrie Morse and Joe Dustin.*

bottom   *Lucio Agostini, Dr. Goldsmith and Andrew Allan.*

Photos show people involved with series "The Ways of Mankind" which was adapted by Sinclair, produced by Allan and sponsored by the Ford Foundation. The series was considered the best radio series on primitive peoples ever produced.

Sir Thomas Beecham who agreed to work for Harry at only $400 a show as a long-hair disc jockey.

Harry started his career as a farm broadcaster at CKNX Wingham, and has continued to pursue his own ideas through an astonishing series of careers as radio writer, producer, executive producer, radio executive, television-executive producer and now as the Vice-President of the Canadian Radio Television Commission. He has always maintained a policy of helping the down-and-out and encouraging the young, and if he seems to believe in God, himself and the underdog in that order, it's because this philosophy has never failed him — so far it has always got the job done.

Earlier in this book I stated that in my opinion the CBC has served its listeners better than any other system in the world. In a country whose population is so far-flung, where else could people with no access to big-city theatre have depended on radio to bring some of the world's greatest dramas, into their homes?

Andrew Allan was the man who was mainly responsible for bringing excellent radio drama to Canadians during the Golden Age. His drama series, "Stage 44" which began in 1944 and ran for years was one of the most consistently excellent drama series ever produced in North America, running the theatrical gauntlet from the "classics" to original plays through to hilarious political satires.

The man behind this Stage series was once described by Lister Sinclair as a "great Victorian" or a man who combined learning with authority. He also had a reputation as a slave-driver but no one denied that he was the best producer in English radio. Allan could be a bully, guardian angel, a mother, a father and a holy terror depending on what he felt was needed at the time. As well as being a great producer he was one of Canada's ablest radio writers and he successfully adapted many of Shakespeare's plays for radio.

Drama critics in both Canada and the United States, excited by the Stage series, suggested that Allan's radio plays should be considered models for other producers to follow. Allan's success largely depended on a talented colony of actors he had helped create to perform the plays written by his writers. This gave tremendous freedom to the writers who could write anything they wanted secure in the knowledge that Allan would have actors who could perform the parts well. Excellent plays produced by Allan during the Golden Age were "Burlap Bags" by Len Petersen and Ted Allan's "The Basketweavers" — dramas with strong social comment. "The Investigator," a spoof on "McCarthyism" was so good that illegal records of the play were sold under the counter in New York, and his production of "Mr. Arcularis" became a classic radio play that was reproduced year after year to enchanted audiences.

If Allan was partial to productions of English classics featuring actors with mid-Atlantic accents (half-way between English and Canadian) it was Esse Ljungh, a fierce Canadian nationalist, who was Allan's chief competitor in radio drama. Esse had a passion — he wanted to develop Canadian authors to write drama for Canadian actors.

CANADIAN BROADCASTING CORPORATION

 Friendly rivals, Esse Ljungh and Andrew Allan, at 25th anniversary party for CBC Stage.

Esse's sense of showbiz also allowed him to produce slick, smooth and effective stories without getting hung up on the traditions or conventions in radio drama. His production of Orwell's "1984" was a complex technical feat

134

"Jake and the Kid" starred John Drainie (left) as Jake, Jack Mather (centre) as Weigh Freight Brown and Frank Peddie as Old Man Gatenby.

produced by Esse for its radio effect only; he didn't care whether the "egghead" magazines approved of his adaptation from the book. Essentially "commercial" in his productions, Esse always had a large following of fans.

In retrospect it seems to me that in those great days radio was producing dramas for almost every taste. Frank Willis's production "The Days of Sail" a collection of salty epics written by Joseph Schull about the East Coast sailing fleet including some adventures of the Bluenose, was remembered with such affection by radio listeners that Frank repeated the 1953 scripts in 1969.

For farm listeners, Summer Fallow an anthology series of farm-oriented dramas was produced in various centres across the country, and the shows from Halifax, Winnipeg and Vancouver were excellent. Science fiction fans could listen to Rod Coneybeare's show "Out of this World" and prairie audiences were treated to Bill Mitchell's "Jake and the Kid!" Oddly enough the show was very popular all across Canada except on the Prairies where the listeners thought Mitchell was caricaturing them. I worked on this particular series and used to regard it as the highlight of my week probably because I realized, along with the rest of the group involved, that it was one of the best series ever produced in Canada. For Canada's movie fans, Ford Radio Theatre produced movie stories adapted for radio on Friday nights. There was also Buckingham Radio Theatre "poor man's radio theatre" or good popular drama developed for mass taste. The series depended on stories and scripts bought from famous authors throughout the world and included writers like Paul Gallico, Somerset Maugham and Agatha Christie.

Canada has always had a well-deserved reputation for producing good documentary dramas. It was Esse Ljungh who developed the CBC style of drama documentary designed to reveal a problem rather than suggest solutions. Maybe Ljungh cottoned on early to the realization that Canadians, unlike their American neighbours have always taken a more serious view of life. To develop that idea a little further we might say that while the Americans are reading the *Joy of Sex* Canadians are reading *Gray's Anatomy*. No matter what the reason one of the first of these documentaries, "In Search of Ourselves" which was first produced in 1946 became so popular that it ran for nearly seven years. Here are the subjects of some of the shows that Canadians could not resist — alcoholism, drug addiction, pre-marital sex, women in prison — any subject which dealt with mental stress. Dr. John Griffin, Director of the National Committee for Mental Hygiene, guided the series and frequently appeared on the program as well. The creators of the series hoped that listeners with the same problems would be persuaded to seek professional help, and that some of the social stigma attached to these particular problems would be eased.

Cross Section was another documentary series which concerned itself with such subjects as economic advice, education, health and labour relations, and "Ways of Mankind" was an anthropological series sponsored by the Ford Foundation and largely written by Lister Sinclair who crops up throughout Canada's radio history as an expert on practically everything.

The Golden Age of radio was a time when children listened to the radio as avidly as they now watch TV. A lot of us can probably still remember the days when we did our homework to the sound of hoofs beating a tattoo across open plains while a voice cried out, "Hi Ho Silver." Maybe some readers will even remember "Men in Scarlet" a commercial series produced during the war by Lowney's Chocolate. Remember Sergeant Pearce riding on horseback across our vast prairies, *"tlot, tlot, neigh"* . . . mushing by dogsled through our frozen northland, *"mush, bow wow!"* . . . patrolling along our coastal waters, *"putt putt"* . . . flying in planes along the skyways of our great dominion, *"vroooom, vroom"* . . . *"Oh the Men in Scarlet ever on the alert to keep law and order and maintain the right."*

It not only maintained the right it maintained a large audience of kids.

Rod Coneybeare and Charles Winter starred in the outstanding children's show, "The Rod and Charles Show".

Maybe some of the readers even remember Harry Red Foster's pep talks as director of the Lowney Young Canada Club:

> A little boy
> A pair of skates.
> A hole in the ice
> He saw it too late
> The story ends at the Golden Gates.

Children's programs produced during the Golden Age were rich in imagination and fantasy. "Cuckoo Clock House" was one of the best and it was heard on Sunday afternoons. Babs Brown with the help of the librarians at Boys and Girls House of the Toronto Public Library system, wrote the scripts and chose the stories. The "Rod and Charles Show" had as many adult fans as children because of the excellent shows they wrote about exploring the world of science. It was an inspiration of producer Dan McCarthy to put the two well-known children's broadcasters together and Rod Coneybeare and Charles Winter came up with some dazzling ideas. I think their most memorable shows were the ones in which the two men acted out the parts of electrons and other scientific materials and then gave impressions of experiments from the inside-out so to speak.

Byng
Whittecker

Byng Whitteker produced fine jazz shows like "Moonmist" (above).

Three other longstanding children's programs were "Just Mary," "Maggie Muggins" and "Kindergarten of the Air." Kindergarten of the Air started in 1947 for mid-eastern Canada and extended to full network in 1948. Dorothy Jane Goulding (Mrs. William Needles) was the teacher, and Sandra Scott played the piano. The program was simplicity itself — one song and one lesson were taught each day. It was a gentle program similar to "Friendly Giant".

Another Vancouver winner was a children's drama series "Magic Adventures" produced by Peter McDonald which won Ohio awards in 1946 and 47. The fantasy stories by Kitty Marcuse were acted out by her friends Don Gaylord and Carolyn Lawrence in The Land of Wog.

A very popular local Toronto children's show was the "Small Types Club" with Byng Whitteker. Whitteker either read stories to the children or played appropriate records ending the program with a long drawn out "Sssssssssccooot! Out to play, back into bed, off to school or whatever mother tells you." On the rare occasions when this formality was omitted

Byng Whitteker with two fans of his children's show "Small Types Club".

Whitteker was told that hundreds of kids had refused to follow their usual routine. But Whitteker was best known as an announcer on Audio and for his jazz programs. A personal friend of many of the jazz greats, Byng had a loyal following of jazz fans for his programs, "Starlight Moods", "Moonmist" and "Thirteen and Terry". In these live jazz concert shows, voices were used as musical instruments intended to blend with the orchestra and the singers were encouraged to sing in low or high registers to give the music strange effects.

Music has always comprised most of the radio schedule in every era but the inherent qualities and sounds of music are difficult to write about. During the 1940s and 1950s there were many excellent musical programs which had large sweeping orchestras, thrilling choirs and magnificent soloists but publishing the lyrics and formats of these programs will really not revive memories. A snatch of an old song, overheard late at night on the car radio is capable of flooding us with much more nostalgia. As I look over the

 The 25 female voices of the Armdale Choir led by Mary Dee soothed listeners of the fifties.

schedules from the Golden Age it does seem however that it was a time when the Leslie Bell Singers from Toronto and the Armdale Chorus from Halifax were extremely popular. The Don Wright Chorus from London, Ontario and the Ivan Romanoff singers on "Songs of My People" were constantly featured, and smaller choral groups like the Four Gentlemen, the Carl Tapscott singers and the Harmony Harbour quartet with its sea songs from Halifax, were also on the air. It was also a period when folk singers began to be featured including old Ed McCurdy, Alan Mills from Montreal and Tony Stecheson or "Tony the Troubadour" as he was known. Fiddle playing was in its heyday in the string orchestras heard from Vancouver, Winnipeg, Toronto, Montreal and Halifax, and country and western music was represented in the East by the Don Messer Show and in the West by the Burn's Chuckwagon and Prairie Schooner shows.

Bert Devitt (with folk singer Malka Himmel) had the sexiest voice on CBC radio.

I remain nostalgic about certain shows like "Escape with Me", a late night show with Bert Devitt who talked to his buddy Smitty, against a background of seagulls and ocean surf pounding the shore. His buddy Smitty (who never talked on the show) was actually a gal, Mary Sime who played the piano for the show. Bert never talked about sex — his stories were always about shipwrecks and jail but listeners still swear it was the sexiest show they ever heard. The Sunshine Society featuring some of the best talent in Toronto was also one of my favourites though nobody else seems to remember the show.

141

Jim Kent
producer

J.B. "Hamish"
Mc Geachy
(moderator)

announcer
Frank Herbert

Dr Boyd
Neel

James
Bannerman

Ralph
Allen

Morley
Callaghan

"Now I Ask You" was a popular radio panel show for eggheads.

In classical music, radio was overwhelmed with talent during the Golden Age. It ranged from Lois Marshall to Glenn Gould and there were many outstanding symphony orchestras and opera choirs. In fact, for several years the CBC maintained the CBC Symphony and a CBC Opera Company which produced outstanding concerts and provided a platform for the development of Canadian musicians and composers. Just as important was the active financial support given by the CBC to orchestras in Winnipeg, Edmonton, Halifax and Vancouver. This support has now been transferred to the Secretary of State department. Pity.

While the Golden Age of radio has its own great moments there were certain constants through all of the ages of Canadian radio — and one of

Quentin McLean played organ for poetry readings on "Nocturne" by Frank Willis.

He Scores! Foster Hewitt's hockey broadcasts made him as national an institution as the game itself.

these was hockey. Canadians first began to listen to their own radio because of Foster Hewitt, and throughout the Second World War the reliability and excitement of Foster's hockey broadcasts continued to dominate the radio scene.

It's hard sometimes for fans to realize that Foster, whose popularity has lasted right up to the present day, has done many other kinds of broadcasting besides hockey. Because his name is so synonymous with the game the rest of his career has been largely forgotten.

Foster began his career as a sports journalist for the *Toronto Star* working for his father on the sports desk. When the paper opened its own radio station CFCA Foster slipped naturally into radio broadcasting, and covering hockey broadcasts was just one of his many chores at the time. He worked for the CNR from time to time on their network covering special events including the arrival of the Empress of Britain in Quebec city. He was also a regular newscaster on CFCA and the fact that he was paid $150 a week while freelancing during the lean thirties is an indication of his reputation.

Hockey became the most popular radio program in Canada during the 1940s and 1950s and has since become the most popular television program. The success of the sport and the broadcasts is a tribute to the broadcasters involved. Yet when it started to go to the network in 1932, the sponsor, General Motors did not feel that the program could hold its audience between periods so they included dance music from The Silver Slipper in Toronto. Later they produced drama sketches during intermissions, and eventually they hit on "The Hot Stove League" with Elmer Ferguson, Wes McKnight and Court Benson discussing the game. Another institution that survived from the 1930s to this day is the 3-Star Selection inspired by "3-Star Gasoline" advertised on the broadcast. For years Foster started the broadcast after his introduction from Charles Jennings with "Hello Canada and hockey fans in the United States and Newfoundland." During the war he also greeted "our men overseas" and on one occasion when it was known that the Germans were tranmitting the hockey game to our troops in Belgium and Holland along with the pitch from a Nazi female broadcaster "Why not call off the war and go home to see the hockey games", Foster added on the Christmas broadcast, "and an extra big hello to Calamity Jane of Arnhem." It seems somehow fitting that as we come to the end of Canada's Golden age in radio we close with the story of Foster Hewitt, the man who was in at some of the beginnings of that history.

Signing Off

Television killed radio but it wasn't a clean kill. Radio was abandoned piece by piece in Canada as listeners switched their loyalty to the picture box and the CBC was forced to spend money and effort in enormous quantities on the family's baby. The Dominion network officially ended the summer of 1962 but the actual death was closer to 1958. The major cities of Canada by then had television and the sponsors and audiences were bewitched by the tube. Although radio staffers in the private sector had begun to make plans for a switch-over to TV as early as 1952 and a lot of CBC people were also thinking hard about the new medium, there were many who believed that the novelty of watching TV would finally wear off. It never happened.

By the time that radio staff had discovered TV viewers would watch inferior material on the box in preference to good material on radio, the impact of the cost of television had set in. Money was going to be short and since television needed a lot of supervision that's where the money would go. Also most of the good radio shows had gone to TV including "Westinghouse Presents", "Hockey Night in Canada" and "The Wayne and Shuster Show". As TV completely covered a large part of the country more and more sponsors dropped radio advertising and concentrated on television. Also by 1959 there were no American radio shows available for networking. Radio didn't really die — listeners and sponsors just walked away from it.

It was a bitter time for those who believed in radio. In the private sector the death of radio wasn't quite so painful because most of the staff transferred to television or became management executives. Some radio stations refused to acknowledge the end of the era — CBM in Montreal as well as CJAD haven't changed that much in twenty years. CFRB hung in with some of

147

its program ideas and most of its personalities including Jack Dennett, Wally Crouter, Wishart Campbell, Jack Dawson, John Collingwood Reade, Wes McKnight and of course, Gordon Sinclair. When CFRB finally gave in to the disc-jockey concept, instead of pocketing the "talent" budget they created the Canadian Talent Library which is a non-profit organization owned by Standard Broadcasting. Canadian Talent Library produces and records Canadian musicians and singers on LP transcriptions and makes them available without profit to all radio stations including CBC. With the advent of the Canadian content quotas for radio this library was a godsend to radio-station owners. It had been a godsend to the performers long before that.

In the CBC the radio staff became angry at seeing the money TV used and, in our opinion, wasted. Producers who used to run their programs on verbal contracts suddenly had new "forms" to fill out which ended personal relationships. Our first reaction was blunt refusal and we hung out for about five months as I recall. Performers who had been delighted to earn $40 for a radio part were now looking at $100 or $200 for a similar role in TV. Radio performers who used to work five to eight hours a day in radio discovered they could get five hours of radio and eight of TV, hence more money. If a conflict arose between radio and television they took TV because the total amount of work and dollars came to much more. Most actors and radio performers agonized over their loyalties. Over the years the performers' association with the radio producers had been one of respect and mutual admiration; TV disrupted this relationship. Many of the actors who were not versatile enough to play innumerable radio parts were ideally suited to the typecasting that TV viewers preferred. Translated to the radio colony this meant that the "failures" were becoming "stars" while many "successes" in radio were "failures" in TV.

Our friends in TV called us the "blind" service. At two Christmas parties in a row there were fights between radio and TV technicians and senior CBC management in an effort to raise the morale of radio staff declared radio the "senior service". Many radio production supervisors, who had limited responsibilities, spent their evenings watching TV. They were never forgiven.

By 1957 all of the big radio variety shows were gone, the Happy Gang was falling apart, dramas had budgets cut from $1000 per half hour to $300, and orchestras were cut to quartets or trios or even replaced with records on some drama series. Writers could no longer afford to write for radio drama productions. The CBC Symphony and Opera companies were then cut back, and good or expensive productions were moved to the daytime schedule by being "double exposed" and eventually the evening productions were dropped in favour of daytime programs.

But we were producing good programs despite all of these cutbacks. John Reeves was producing a good drama series "Four's Company," composers

148

like Harry Freedman were putting out excellent stuff, and drama critic Nathan Cohen was becoming nationally known on radio. But no matter how good the programs were they could not attract the audiences who were watching TV.

Radio did make one significant change when the impact of smaller audiences was understood. While talks and public affairs shows had always appealed to the university crowd many of the other programs were also refashioned for "eggheads". Teenagers also became a major factor in radio programming because of their addiction to popular music and the Action Set on Saturday morning was an excellent project, set up for teenage audiences. Television had broken some CBC taboos regarding travel programs and this created an opportunity for Harry Boyle to develop his "Project" series, radio travel documentaries reporting from around the world. Perhaps their biggest scoop was an interview with Fidel Castro in the moutains of Cuba shortly before he took control of the country.

The churches decided that a plain old church service was not the way to get the "message" across and many of the clergy asked to become involved in more meaningful religious programming. Unfortunately some of the new programs were considered too radical and there are many of the clergy who still prefer the more old-fashioned approach. But private radio stations still earn a considerable part of their income from religious programming.

As I look back on my own career in radio, it seems to me now that it was a fourteen-year odyssey in which I pursued my own private dream about radio. Even when it was obvious that there was no way the dreams could be made into a reality I couldn't give them up. I kept trying to beat television with programs like Audio on CJBC and Assignment which I collaborated on with Harry Boyle. I even retreated to areas without television like the North West Territories where I set up radio stations and from there to Jamaica where there was still a chance for mass audience radio.

Eventually as I grew older, wiser and sadder, I made the transfer into television where I have worked for thirteen years travelling constantly across Canada in TV production and always loyally listening to the radio. I realize now that I was lucky to spend part of my life working in Canadian radio during its best days and I also know that those days can never return. We had great times and a lot of fun and now it's time to sign off. Goodbye out there in radioland.

149

Bibliography

Allan, Andrew. *Andrew Allan; a self portrait.* Toronto: Macmillan of Canada, 1975.

Allen, Fred. *Treadmill to oblivion.* Boston: Little, Brown, 1954.

Baker, W. J. *The History of the Marconi Company.* London: Methuen, 1970.

Barnouw, Erik. *Handbook of radio production.* Boston: Little, Brown, 1949.

Briggs, Asa. *The history of broadcasting in the United Kingdom.* London: Oxford University Press, 1961.

Buxton, Frank. *The big broadcast, 1920-1950.* New York: Viking Press, 1972.

Canada. House of Commons. *Special committee on radio broadcasting. Minutes of proceedings and evidence.* Ottawa: King's Printer, 1932.

Canada. *Royal Commission on Broadcasting. Report, March 15, 1957.* Ottawa: Queen's Printer, 1957. Chairman: Robert M. Fowler.

Canada. *Royal Commission on National Development in the Arts, Letters and Sciences, 1949-51. Broadcasting in Canada, radio and television.* Ottawa: King's Printer, 1951. Chairman: Vincent Massey.

Canada. *Royal Commission on Radio Broadcasting. Report.* Ottawa: King's Printer, 1929. Chairman: Sir John Aird.

Canada. *Special Senate Committee on Mass Media. Report.* Ottawa: Queen's Printer, 1970. Chairman: Keith Davey.

Canada. *Task force on labour relations. Broadcasting, an industry study,* by Ruby S. Samlalsingh. Ottawa: Queen's Printer, 1968.

Canadian Broadcasting Corporation. *Chronology of network broadcasting in Canada, 1901-1961.* Compiled by A. J. Black. Ottawa: Canadian Broadcasting Corporation, 1961.

Canadian Broadcasting Corporation. *Five years of achievement;* a series of illustrated pamphlets describing the work of the CBC in its principal aspects since November, 1936. Toronto: Canadian Broadcasting Corporation. n.d.

Canadian Broadcasting Corporation. *Handbook for announcers.* Toronto: Canadian Broadcasting Corporation, 1946.

Canadian Broadcasting Corporation. *CBC regulations for broadcasting stations and extracts from the Canadian Broadcasting Act, 1936.* Canadian Broadcasting Corporation, 1941.

The Canadian Radio Yearbook, 1947-48. Hugh S. Newton, editor. Toronto, 1947.

Corbett, Edward A. *We have with us tonight.* Toronto: Ryerson Press, 1957.

Dunlap, Orrin E. *The story of radio.* New York: Dial Press, 1935.

Edmondson, Madeline, and Rounds, David. *Soaps: daytime serials of radio and television.* New York: Stein and Day, 1973.

Goldschmidt, Walter, ed. *Ways of mankind:* thirteen dramas of people of the world and how they live, by Lister Sinclair, Len Peterson, Eugene S. Hallman, George Salverson. Boston: Beacon Press, 1954.

Gruneau Research Ltd. *A survey of Canadian public opinion towards radio and the CBC.* Toronto: Gruneau Research Ltd., 1952.

Harmon, Jim. *The great radio comedians.* New York: Doubleday, 1970.

Harmon, Jim. *The great radio heroes.* New York: Doubleday, 1967.

Herron, Edward Albert. *Miracle of the air waves; a history of radio.* Messner, 1969.

Higby, Mary Jane. *Tune in tomorrow; or, how I found The Right to Happiness with Our Gal Sunday, Stella Dallas, John's Other Wife, and other sudsy radio serials.* New York: Cowles, 1968.

Irving, John A., ed. *Mass media in Canada.* Toronto: Ryerson, 1962.

Kendrick Alexander. *Prime Time: the life of Edward R. Murrow.* Boston: Little, Brown, 1969.

Koch, Howard. *The panic broadcast; portrait of an event.* Boston: Little, Brown, 1970.

Jackson, Roger Lee. *An historical and analytical study of the origin, development and impact of the dramatic programs produced for the English language networks of the Canadian Broadcasting Corporation.* Ann Arbor: University Microfilms, 1967. Ph.D. Thesis, Wayne State University.

Jamieson, Donald Campbell. *The troubled air.* Fredericton: Brunswick Press, 1966.

Lackman, Ron. *Remember radio.* New York: Putnam, 1970.

Lambert, Richard Stanton. *School broadcasting in Canada.* Toronto: University of Toronto Press, 1963.

Mitchell, Curtis. *Cavalcade of broadcasting.* Chicago: Follett, 1970.

Palmer, B. J. *Radio salesmanship.* 6th ed. Tri-City Broadcasting Company, Inc., 1947.

Peers, Frank Wayne. *The politics of Canadian Broadcasting, 1920-1951.* Toronto: University of Toronto Press, 1969.

Powley, A. E. *Broadcast from the front; Canadian radio overseas in the second world war.* Toronto: Hakkert, 1975.

Raby, Ormond. *Radio's first voice: the story of Reginald Fessenden.* Toronto: Macmillan of Canada, 1970.

Seldes, Gilbert. *The public arts.* New York: Simon and Schuster, 1956.

Settel, Irving. *A pictorial history of radio.* New York: Citadel Press, 1960.

Sinclair, Lister. *A play on words and other radio plays.* Toronto: Dent, 1948.

Stursberg, Peter. *Mister broadcasting: the Ernie Bushnell story.* Toronto: Peter Martin, 1971.

Thomas, Lowell. *Magic dials; the story of radio and television.* New York: Polygraph Company of America, 1939.

Walter, Arnold, ed. *Aspects of music in Canada.* Toronto: University of Toronto Press, 1969.

Weir, E. Austin. *The struggle for national broadcasting in Canada.* Toronto: McClelland and Stewart, 1965.

Miscellaneous

Actra. Spring, 1967.

Face to face with talent. 1973 ed. Toronto: Association of Canadian Television and Radio Artists.

Canadian Broadcasting Corporation. *CBC, a brief history and background.* 1972.

Canadian Broadcasting Corporation. *This is the CBC, your national radio system.*

CBC Times. July, 1948 - December, 1969.

CBC Program Schedules.

CFRB 10th anniversary yearbook, 1937.

CFRB 25th anniversary booklet.

Encyclopedia Canadiana, 1968.

Financial Post. May 22, 1943. Eight page section on private radio.

Maclean's. Feb. 1, 1950

Manitoba Calling. 1937-1948. Winnipeg: Manitoba Telephone System.

Momentous years with CFRB, 1927-1957. recording.

Music, '49-'50. Publicity pamphlet for CBC "Wednesday Night".

Personalities in radioland. Toronto: DeForest Crosley Ltd., 1931.

Radio; CBC staff magazine. 1944-1952.

Radio Digest. May 3, 1924.

Radio guide; the national weekly of programs and personalities. Jan. 9, 1932.

Radio World. Oct. 7, 1944, Mar. 30, 1946, Apr. 16, 1946.

Spry, Graham. *Public policy and private pressure: The Canadian Radio League 1930-6 and countervailing power in Canada;* essays in honour of Frank H. Underhill, edited by Norman Penlington. Toronto: University of Toronto Press, 1971. pp. 24-36.

Willis, J. Frank. Programs produced and directed by, Sept. 1939-Oct. 1969. Compiled by Grace Athersich.

INDEX

(Figures in italics refer to illustrations)

Adaskin, John, 97, 108
Agostini, Guiseppe, 45, 92
Agostini, Lucio, 81, 113, *132*
Aird, Sir John, 22
Aird Commission (Royal Commission on Radio Broadcasting 1929), 22, 23, 41
Aitken, Kate, 109, *110, 121*
Albert, Norman, 44
Alden, Iris, 79
Allen, Eddie, 125, *127*
Allan, Andrew, 63, *85*, 102, *105*, 107, 110, 111, 113, *130, 132*, 133, *134*
Allen, Fred, *48*
Anderson, Rolly, 33
Arlington, Virginia, 4
Armdale Choir, *140*
Atlantic Nocturne, 53, *143*
Audio, 139, 149

B. A. Oil, 79
Bartlett, Hugh, 125
A Beach of Strangers, 130
Beaudet, Jean Marie, 73
Beddoes, Dick, 44
Bell, Leslie, 78, *112*, 140
Bennett, R. B., 24
Bergen, Edgar, *48*
"Bert Anstice and his Mountaineers", 47
Billy Bartlett of the Double Bar U, 64
Blanc, Mel, 61
Blattnerphone, *84*
Bochner, Lloyd, 78
Bond, Roxanna, 81
Borden, Robert, 6, 30
Borden's Canadian Cavalcade, 81
Bowman, Bob, 71
Bowman, Charles, 22
Boyle, Harry, 84, 130, *131*, 132, 133, 149
Braden, Bernie, 92, 128
Braithwaite, Max, 78
Brant Rock, 1, *3*, 6, 7, 9
Brave Voyage, 103, 111, *119*
Bushnell, Ernie, 83
Bytown Troubadours, 39

CBM, 147
CFCA, 145
CFCX, 21
CFCY, 43
CFRB, 85, 86, 95, 102, *120*, 128, 147, 148
CHNS, 47
CJAD, 147
CJBC, 21
CKNC, 85
CKNX, 132
CKX, 21

CKY, 21, 85
CNR, 20, *30, 31, 32, 33, 34, 35, 36, 37, 38, 39*, 40, 41, 43, *53*, 93, 98, 99
CNRA, 40
CNRE, 40
CNRV, 102
Cable, Howard, 78, 81
Cameron, Earl, 68
Canadian Broadcast League, 26
Canadian Broadcasting Corporation, 26, 43, 51, 55, 67, 68, 70, 71, 72, 75, 80, 81, 82, 83, 84, 85, 86, 87, 88, 89, 90, 91, 92, 93, 94, 95, 103, 104, 107, 109, 110, 111, 113, 114, 128, 131, 133, 134, 136, 141, 142, 147, 148
Canadian Radio Broadcasting Commission, *24, 25*, 41, 44, 47, 68, 93, 99
Canadian Talent Library, 148
Canadian Theatre of the Air, 86
Canning, Arleigh, *31*, 47
Caplan, Rupert, 63, 111
Cardin, P. J. A., 22
Carry on Canada, 73, 76
The Carsons, 83
Chamberlain, Charlie, 47
Charlesworth, Hector, 24, 25, 26
Christie, Bob, 85, 102
Christmas, Eric, 128
Citizen's Forum, 93
Clark, Greg, 72
Coats, Darby, *20*, 29
Cobb Island, 4
Coldwell, M. J., *92*
Cole, Norman, 40
Command Performance, 80
Coneybeare, Rod, 108, 135, *137*
Coulton, John, 75
The Craigs, 83, 103, 104
Cross, Milton, *88*, 90
Cuckoo Clock House, 137

Dale, Terry, 78
Days of Sail, 135
Deirdre of the Sorrows, 89
Denison, Merrill, 40, 41
Dennis, June, *110*
Devitt, Bert, 109, *141*
Diamond Jubilee July 1, 1927, 39
Diespecker, Dick, 76
Dominion Network, 95, 114, 147
Dominion Observatory Time Signal, 40
Drainie, John, *61*, 64, 78, 85, 113, *135*
Drew, George, *70*
Dunton, Davidson, 93

Eckstein, Willie, 29
Edison, Thomas Alva, 2

Edwards, Lloyd, 126, *127*
Escape With Me, 109, *141*

Faith, Percy, 73, 92
Farnon, Bob, *124*, 125
Fessenden, Reginald, frontis, 1, 2, 3, 4, 5, 7, 9, 11
Fessenden Wireless Telegraph Co. of Canada, 6
Fibber McGee and Molly, 82
Fighting Navy, 64, 78
First Broadcast, 1, 9
Ford Radio Theatre, 100, *109*, 113, 136
Forgotten Footsteps, 44
Forsee, Reid, *102*, 109
Foster, Harry Red, 80, 137
Foster, Les, 126, *127*
Four Continental Porters, *37*, 40
Frigon, August, 22
Fuller, Jack, 78, 79

Gauthier, Eva, 39
General Electric Showtime, 110, 113
General Motors, 19, 44
"George Wade and his Cornhuskers", 47
Ghostwalkers, 44
Gibbs, Terence, 111
The Gillans, 83
Gimby, Bobby, 124, 126, *127*
Goffman, Francis, 79
Goossens, Eugene, 73
Gott, Herb, 79, 105
Gould, Mona, *110*
Goulding, Dorothy Jane, 138
Grannan, Mary, *93*, 94
Greene, Lorne, 68, *69*, 80
Grosart, Alistar, 80
Guthrie, Tyrone, 40, 41, 98

Halton, Matthew, 55, 71, *75*
Happy Gang, 108, 113, 123, *124*, *125*, *126*, *127*, 148
Harris, Alf, 65
Hart House String Quartet, 39, *90*, 91
Henshaw, Don, 44
Hersenhoren, Samuel, 76, 92
Hertz, Heinrich, 3
Hewitt, Foster, *18*, 19, 41, 44, *144*, 145
Higgins, Howard, 79
Hill, Gus, 29, 30, 31
Hockey broadcasts, 18, 19, 44, 144, 145, 147
Hockridge, Ted, 78
Holmes, Art, 56, *70*, 71
Hopper, Bert, 25
Hopkins, Len, 92
The Hot Stove League, 145
Hughes, Dean, 83

The Investigator, 133

The Jacksons, 83
Jake and the Kid, 63, 113, *135*
James, Frances, 91
Jarvis St. Baptist Church, 21
Jehovah's Witness, 21, 22, 25
Jennings, Charles, 68, 145
John and Judy, 81
Johnny Home Show, 128
Jordan, Charlie, 93
Juliette, 92
Just Mary, 93, 94, 138

KDKA, *14*, *15*
Kannawin, John, 72, 108
Kennedy, Syd, 43
Kenney, Mart, *79*, 92
King, Mackenzie, 24, 26, 27, 30, 67, 87, 110
Knapp, Bud, *60*
Ku Klux Klan, 22

L for Lanky, 79
Lafleche, Giselle, 78
LaFleur, Benoit, *70*, 71, 72
LaFleur, Joy, *60*
Landry, Cecil, 47
Lanphier, Father, 87
Lapp, Horace, 92, 109
The Last Voyage of Henry Hudson, 40
Let's Make Music, *107*, 108
Ljungh, Esse, 44, 63, 85, *106*, *108*, 110, 111, 113, *119*, 130, 133, *134*, 137
Lockerbie, Beth, *106*
Loder, Peggi, 78, *119*
Lucas, Clarence, 40
Lucas, Rupert, 26, 75, 85, 103
Lutton, Dorothy, 30, 31
Lux Radio Theatre, 100

Ma Perkins, 80
Macbeth, Madge, *39*
Machrihanish, 6, 7
Mack, Cy, 81
MacMillan, Ernest, 40, 73, 81, 82
McArthur, Dan, 68
McCarthy, Dan, 137
McDermott, A. A., 76
McFee, Alan, 65
McGeachy, J. B. (Hamish), 72
McIntyre, James, *38*
McKay, Cliff, 124, 126
McKlintock, Bill, 63
McLean, Quentin, *143*
McLeod, Mercer, 44, 78
McNeil, Corby, 79
McQuhae, Alan, 39
Maher, Thomas, 24
Mallett, Jane, 105

Manitoba Telephone Company, 29, 85
Manson, Donald, 29
Marconi Company in Canada, 15, 29, 31, 79
Marconi, Guglielmo, 1, *2*, *3*, *6*, *8*, *9*, 11, *12*, 15
Markle, Fletcher, 76, 85
Martin, Art, 79
Mathe, Blain, *124*, 125
Mather, Jack, *135*
Maxted, Stanley, 44
Men in Scarlet, 136
Mendelssohn Choir, 90, 91
Messer, Don, *46*, 47, 140
Messiah, 91
Metropolitan Opera, 45, 88, 90
Milsom, Howard, 78
Minifie, James M., 72
Mr. Arcularis, 133
Mr. Sage, 26
Mitchell, W. O. (Bill), 113, 135
Monnier, Madeleine, 40
Moonie, Esmé, 41
Moose River Mine, 47, *50, 51*
Murray, George, 79

Namaro, Jimmy, 126, *127*
National Electric Signalling Co., 5, 6
Needles, Bill, 81
Niosi, Bert, 126
Niosi, Joe, 126, *127*
Now I Ask You, 142
Noxon, Gerald, 80

One Hour With You, 45
One Man's Family, 86
Opportunity Knocks, *61*, 108
Ouimet, Marcel, 55, *70*, 71

Paige, Wendy, 110
Parker, Pete, 44
Pearl, Bert, 108, 123, *124, 125, 126, 127*
Peddie, Frank, 104, 106, 135
Peterson, Len, 113, 133
Poldhu, Cornwall, 1
Powley, Bert, 71, 72
Pratz, Albert, 92, 108
Purdy, Rai, 81, 85, 102

Radio telephony, 1
Rae, Jackie, 65, 78, 109, 110
Rae, John, 78, 123
Reeves, John, 130, 148
Rennie, Pauline, 79
Roach, Bill, 65
Robb, J., 38, 40
The Rod and Charles Show, 137
The Romance of Canada, 40, 98

Rosen, Al, *64*
Royal Tour, 1939, 51, *66, 67*, 91

Salverson, George, 78, 113
Sandwell, B. K., 93
Sarnoff, David, 12, 13
Savage, David, 83
Sheridan, Alex, *62*
Shugg, Orville, 83, 84
Shuster, Frank, 77, *78*, 79, 108, 113, 128, *129*, 147
Signal Hill, St. John's, 1, *8*
Sims, Don, 93
Sinclair, Gordon, *121*, 148
Sinclair, Lister, 63, 78, *130, 132*, 133, 136
"The Singing Lumberjacks", 47
Slade, Ted, 61
Sliz, John, 60, *63, 64*
Small Types Club, 138
Smith, Max, 29
Snider, Lou, 94, 109, 126
Soldier's Wife, 81
Stage, 113, 133, 134
Stanley, Bert, 52, *61*, 63, 65
Steel, Lt. Col. W. Arthur, 24
Stokes, Kay, *123, 124, 125, 126*
Strange, Bill, 64, 76, 78, 113
Strange, Cy, 109, *121*
Stursburg, Peter, 71, 75
Surdin, Morris, 128
Symes, Harold, 52, 63

Tanner, Gord, 52, 63
Tasker, Dave, *60*
Texaco, 88, 90
Theatre of Freedom, 75
They Fly For Freedom, 80
Thornton, Sir Henry, 38, 40, 41
Titanic, 10, 11, *12*, 13
Titus, Russ, 79
Toronto Star, *41*, 145
Tovell, Vincent, 78, 79
Trans Canada Network, 95, 114, 131
Transcription services, 117
Transit Through Fire, 75
Tudor, Fred, 52, 63
Tweed, Tommy, 44, 85, 104, 130

Upton, Jules, 79

Waddington, Geoff, 92, 97
Wadsworth, Harold, 71, 72
Wallace, Clair, 95
War of the Worlds, 54
Wasserman, Charles, 113
Wayne, Johnny, 77, *78*, 79, 108, 113, 128, *129*, 147
Ways of Mankind, *132*, 136